QuickBooks®
5.0
for Accounting

Glenn Owen
Allan Hancock College

Paul Solomon
San Jose State University

D1511419

South-Western College Publishing
an International Thomson Publishing company I(T)P®

Cincinnati • Albany • Boston • Detroit • Johannesburg • London • Madrid • Melbourne • Mexico City
New York • Pacific Grove • San Francisco • Scottsdale • Singapore • Tokyo • Toronto

Publishing Team Director: Richard Lindgren
Sponsoring Editor: David L. Shaut
Production Editor: Barbara Fuller Jacobsen
Production House: DPS Associates, Inc.
Multimedia Production Editor: Lora Craver
Internal Design: Imbue Design
Cover Design: Michael H. Stratton
Cover Photo: © 1997 PhotoDisc
Senior Marketing Manager: Sharon Oblinger

Library of Congress Cataloging-in-Publication data
Owen, Glenn.
    QuickBooks 5.0 for accounting / Glenn Owen, Paul Solomon.
        p.   cm.
    Includes index.
    ISBN 0-324-00357-9
    1. Quickbooks.   2. Accounting—Computer programs.   3. Small
business—Accounting—Computer programs. 4. Small business–
–Finance—Computer programs.   I. Solomon, Paul
II. Title.
HF5679.095   1998   98-24635
657'.9042'2855369—dc21   CIP

I(T)P®

International Thomson Publishing
South-Western College Publishing is an ITP Company.
The ITP trademark is used under license

ISBN 0-324-00402-8 (package)
ISBN 0-324-00357-9 (text only)
ISBN 0-324-00399-4 (data disk only)

1 2 3 4 5 6 7 8 WST 5 4 3 2 1 0 9 8

Printed in the United States of America

Brief Contents

Contents

What if you could integrate a popular computerized accounting program into your classroom without using confusing and complicated manuals? What if your students could use this program and reinforce basic accounting concepts in an online and interactive case setting? What if you could accomplish both without spending a fortune and a vast amount of time preparing examples, cases, and illustrations? In fact, *Quickbooks 5.0 for Accounting* by Owen and Solomon is a textbook that fulfills and expands upon all three of these "what ifs."

WHY IS THIS TEXTBOOK NEEDED?

The first course in accounting has evolved significantly over the last five years. Educators are responding to the demand of accounting and non-accounting faculty who rely on this course to lay a foundation for other courses. Moreover, the accounting profession relies on this course to attract the "best and the brightest" to become accounting majors. The evolution of this course has also put pressure on instructors to integrate computers into the classroom and, in doing so, develop students' skills in intelligently using and interpreting accounting information.

Faculty often want to incorporate computerized accounting into the first course, but are reluctant to invest the time and effort necessary to accomplish this laudable goal. Existing materials are often "preparer" driven in that they focus on the creation of financial reports only. Students' are often discouraged in their use of computers in the first accounting course because of the complicated and confusing accounting software manuals that concentrate on accounting mechanics.

This text responds to all of these needs. It provides a self-paced, step-by-step environment in which students use *QuickBooks 5.0 for Windows* to create financial statements and other financial reports, to reinforce the concepts they learn in their first course, and to see how computer software can be used to make business decisions. The text and problems in *QuickBooks 5.0 for Accounting* have been fully updated from Version 4.0 to reflect any changes.

WHAT ARE THE GOALS OF THIS TEXTBOOK?

This textbook takes a user perspective by illustrating how accounting information is both used and created. QuickBooks is extremely user friendly and provides point and click simplicity with excellent and sophisticated accounting reporting and analysis tools. The textbook uses a proven and successful pedagogy to demonstrate the software's features and elicit student interaction.

The text's first and foremost goal is to help students learn or review fundamental accounting concepts and principles through the use of QuickBooks and the analysis of business events. The content complements the first course in accounting and, therefore, should be used in conjunction with a core text on accounting.

A second goal is to enable students to view financial statements from a user perspective. After an initial tour of QuickBooks, students learn how to use QuickBooks to understand and interpret financial statements.

A third goal of the text is to provide students a means to investigate the underlying source documents that generate most financial accounting information, such as purchase orders, sales invoices, and so on. Students will experience this process by entering a few business events for later inclusion in financial reports.

A fourth goal of the text is to provide students a means of exploring some managerial aspects of accounting by performing financial analysis and comparisons. Budgets are created and compared to actual operating results and receivables and payables are aged for analysis of cash management and cash flow projections.

A fifth goal of this text is to reduce the administrative burdens of accounting faculty by providing a self-paced environment, data sets, cases, and a correlation table describing how this text might be used with a variety of popular accounting texts.

WHAT ARE THE KEY FEATURES OF THIS TEXTBOOK?

The key features of this book are:

- The chapters incorporate a continuing, interesting, realistic case— Phoenix Systems Consulting, Inc.—that helps students apply QuickBooks's features and key accounting concepts.

- A tested, proven step-by-step methodology keeps students on track. Students enter data, analyze information, and make decisions all within the context of the case. The text constantly guides students, letting them know where they are in the course of completing their accounting tasks.

- Numerous screen shots include callouts that direct students' attention to what they should look at on the screen. On almost every page in the book, you will find examples of how steps, screen shots, and callouts work together.

- **trouble?** Paragraphs anticipate the mistakes that students are likely to make or problems they are likely to encounter, and help students recover and continue with the chapter. This feature facilitates independent learning and frees instructors to focus on accounting concepts rather than on computer skills.

- With a very few exceptions, QuickBooks does not require the user to record journal entries to record business events. An appendix on debits and credits gives instructors the flexibility to teach journal entries at their discretion. It provides the information necessary for students to make journal entries to record the events described in Chapters 2 through 7.

- Questions begin the end-of-chapter material. They are intended to test students' recall of what they learned in the chapter.

- Chapter Assignments follow the Questions and provide students additional hands-on practice with QuickBooks skills. Some Chapter Assignments are designated by the icon shown here as Internet Assignments. These are optional.

- A continuing Case Problem—JENNINGS & ASSOCIATES, an advertising firm—concludes each chapter. This case has approximately the same scope as the Phoenix chapter case. The Case Problems ask students to apply the same QuickBooks skills they learned in the chapter to this entirely new case.

- The Instructor's Package contains an Instructor's Manual, including solutions to end-of-chapter materials, and master copies of the Student Disks, which contain the practice data files students need to work through the materials.

Information about QuickBooks Software can be found at **owen.swcollege.com**

http://

ABOUT THE AUTHORS

Glenn Owen is a member of Allan Hancock College's Accounting and Business faculty, where he lectures on accounting and information systems. In addition, he is a lecturer at the University of California at Santa Barbara, where he has been teaching accounting and information systems courses since 1980. His professional experience includes a position at Deloitte & Touche and vice-president of finance positions at Westpac Resources, Inc., and Expertelligence, Inc. He is active in the American Accounting Association, where he serves as the webmaster for the Two-Year College section. He has authored many Internet-related books and accounting course supplements and is currently developing on-line accounting instruction modules for his Internet-only based financial accounting courses. His innovative teaching style emphasizes the decision-maker's perspective and encourages students to think creatively. His graduate studies in educational psychology and his 24 years of business experience combine for a balanced blend of theory and practice.

Paul Solomon is Professor Emeritus of Accounting at San Jose State University, where he had been on the faculty for 19 years until his retirement in 1998. His previous faculty positions were at DePaul University—where he received his MBA—and the University of Minnesota—where he received his doctorate. His professional experience includes positions at the General Accounting Office; Touche Ross; Lybrand, Ross Brothers and Montgomery; and Haskins and Sells. Today Dr. Solomon is a leading proponent of implementing a user-oriented first course in accounting and travels extensively to present faculty workshops and to consult with individual accounting programs. While at San Jose State, he was the principal author of the Core Competency Model, a mainstream, user-oriented, active learning, competency-based first course in accounting and chaired for 10 years a conference that became known as the California Colloquium on Accounting Education. He has been very involved in the American Accounting Association's (AAA) new focus on faculty development and, as an individual, has established a national faculty conference—The Colloquium on Change in Accounting Education. These initiatives to champion change in accounting education have earned him the American Accounting Association's 1998 Innovation in Accounting Education Award.

Getting Started with QuickBooks

In this chapter you will:

- **Take an interactive tour of QuickBooks 5.0**

- **Create a balance sheet and modify its presentation**

- **Create an income statement and modify its presentation**

- **Create supporting reports and modify their presentation**

This chapter is designed to help you navigate through QuickBooks 5.0. It provides a foundation for the chapters that follow by showing you how to create a new QuickBooks file and record a variety of operating, investing, and financing transactions.

This chapter is divided into four sessions—each with its own set of Questions, Assignments, and Case Problems. Session 1 of Chapter 1 gives you a quick interactive tour of QuickBooks 5.0, in which you will create your Student Disks and become familiar with QuickBooks's essential features. Sessions 2, 3, and 4 introduce you to creating and preparing the balance sheet, the income statement, and supporting reports.

1

An Interactive Tour of QuickBooks 5.0

Learning Objectives

In this session you will:

- Make your QuickBooks Student Disks
- Launch and exit QuickBooks in Windows 95 or Windows 3.1
- Identify the major components of the QuickBooks window and the major menu commands
- Open and close a QuickBooks file
- Correct mistakes and use the Undo and Revert commands
- Use QuickBooks Help
- View and print a set of financial statements

CASE: ROCK CASTLE CONSTRUCTION COMPANY

You've been working in a part-time job at a restaurant, and today you decide that you've served your last hamburger. You want a new part-time job—one that's more directly related to your future career in business. As you skim the want ads, you see an ad for an administrative assistant at Rock Castle Construction Company. Rock Castle specializes in remodeling existing homes and is well known in town for its quality construction and timely completion of projects. The ad says that job candidates must have earned or be earning a business degree, have some computer skills, and be willing to learn on the job. This looks promising. And then you see the line "Send a resume to Jim Reed." You know Jim Reed! He was in one of your marketing classes two years ago; he graduated last year with a degree in accounting. You decide to send your resume to Jim right away.

A few days later you're delighted to hear Jim's voice on the phone. He remembers you well. He explains that he wants to hire someone to help him with clerical and other administrative tasks in support of his job as Rock Castle's accountant. He asks if you could start right away. When you say yes, he offers you the job on the spot! You start next Monday.

When you arrive Monday morning, Jim explains that the first thing he needs you to learn is how to use a software package called QuickBooks. You quickly remind Jim that you're not an accounting major. Jim laughs as he assures you you'll have no problem with QuickBooks because it is so user oriented. He chose QuickBooks exactly for that reason and has been using it for about six months. Many of the Rock Castle managers want accurate, useful, and timely financial information to help them make sound business decisions, and they're not accountants.

Jim explains that on May 31, 1995 he started using QuickBooks by entering opening balances. Since then, he has recorded all transactions in QuickBooks. But he's becoming so busy at Rock Castle that he now needs someone else in the office who can enter transactions, generate reports for the managers, and so on. So he says that today he will give you a tour of QuickBooks and teach you some of the basic features and functions of this package. You tell him that you're familiar with Windows 3.1 and Windows 95, and you're ready to start.

USING THIS TEXT EFFECTIVELY

Before you begin the tour of QuickBooks, note that this textbook assumes you are familiar with the basics of Windows 3.1 or Windows 95: how to control windows, how to choose menu commands, how to complete dialog boxes, and how to select directories, drives, and files. If you do not understand these concepts, please consult your instructor. Also note that this book is designed to be used with your instructor's and/or another textbook's discussion of essential accounting concepts.

The best way to work through this textbook is to carefully read the text and complete the numbered steps, which appear on a shaded background, as you work at your computer. Read each step carefully and completely before you try it.

As you work, compare your screen with the figures in the chapter to verify your results. You can use QuickBooks 5.0 with either Windows 3.1 or Windows 95. The screen shots you will see in this book were captured in a Windows 95 environment. So if you are using Windows 3.1, you will see some minor differences between your screens and the screens in this book. Any significant differences that result from using the two operating systems with QuickBooks 5.0 will be explained.

Don't worry about making mistakes—that's part of the learning process. The **trouble?** paragraphs identify common problems and explain how to correct them or get back on track. Follow the suggestions *only* if you are having the specific problem described.

After you complete a chapter, you can do the Questions, Assignments, and Case Problems found at the end of each chapter. They are carefully structured so that you will review what you have learned and then apply your knowledge to new situations.

YOUR STUDENT DISKS

To complete the chapters and exercises in this book, you must have a set of Student Disks. The Student Disks contain all the practice files you need for the chapters, the Assignments, and the Case Problems. Your instructor or lab manager may provide you with a set of Student Disks, or your instructor may ask you to make your own Student Disks. To make your own Student Disks, you need four blank formatted high-density disks. You will need to copy a set of files from a file server or standalone computer onto your disks. Your instructor will tell you which computer, drive letter, and folders contain the files you need. The following table shows which files go on each of your disks:

Disk	Put these files on the disk	
Student Disk 1	rock.qbw	kj03cp.qbw
	kj01cp.qbw	phnx03.qbw
	phnx02cp.qbw	
Student Disk 2	phnx03cp.qbw	phnx04cp.qbw
	kj04cp.qbw	phnx05.qbw
	phnx04.qbw	phnx05cp.qbw
Student Disk 3	kj05cp.qbw	phnx06.qbw
	kj06cp.qbw	
Student Disk 4	phnx06cp.qbw	kj07cp.qbw
	phnx07.qbw	

The files on your Student Disks are named to correspond to chapters and sessions in this book. Before using them, copy them (one at a time, as needed) to a blank formatted "working" disk. This will insure that enough space is available on the disk for QuickBooks to temporarily store other data. Keep your original Student Disks unchanged in case you need to start over.

In a business environment, all QuickBooks files would usually be maintained on your computer's hard drive. You are most likely using this book and software in an educational setting, probably a computer lab. Thus, it is necessary for you to maintain your work on multiple disks. Using disks will cause some QuickBooks functions to run more slowly than if you were using a hard drive.

WHAT IS QUICKBOOKS?

Jim is excited about using QuickBooks 5.0 since it is the best selling small business accounting software on the market today (Figure 1.1). He explains that **QuickBooks** is an automated accounting information system that describes an entity's financial position and operating results and that helps managers make more effective business decisions. He also likes QuickBooks's reports and graphs, which quickly and easily organize and summarize all the data he enters.

Jim says he especially likes QuickBooks because it can handle all of Rock Castle's needs to invoice customers and maintain receivables, as well as to pay bills and maintain payables. It can track inventory and create purchase orders using Rock Castle's on-screen forms—all without calculating, posting, or closing. He can correct all transactions he's recorded at any time, while an audit trail feature automatically keeps a record of any changes he makes.

Figure 1.1
The Opening Screen for QuickBooks 5.0

Jim explains further that QuickBooks 5.0 has four basic features that, when combined, help manage the financial activity of a company. The four features—lists, forms, registers, and reports and graphs—work together to create an accounting information system. Let's take a closer look at each of these four features.

Lists

Lists are groups of names, such as customers, vendors, employees, inventory items, and accounts, and information about those names. Lists are created and edited either from a list window or while completing a form, such as an invoice, bill, or time sheet. Figure 1.2 shows a list of Rock Castle's customer names with jobs for each of these customers, balances owed for each job, and any explanatory notes.

Forms

Forms are QuickBooks's electronic representations of the paper documents used to record business activities, such as customer invoices, a vendor's bill for goods purchased, or a check written to a vendor. The

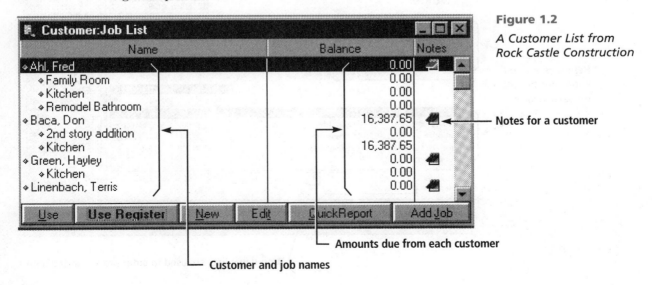

Figure 1.2
A Customer List from Rock Castle Construction

Notes for a customer

Amounts due from each customer

Customer and job names

customer invoice form in Figure 1.3 contains many **fields**, or areas on the form that you can fill in.

If you fill in a field, such as the Customer:Job field, QuickBooks often automatically fills in several other fields with relevant information to speed up data entry. In Figure 1.3, for example, the BILL TO, TERMS, and Tax fields are filled in as soon as the Customer:Job field is entered.

Also, filling in a field is made easier through the use of drop-down lists. Whenever you see an arrow next to or in a field, that field is a drop-down list.

Registers

A QuickBooks **register** contains all financial activity for a specified balance sheet account. Examples of registers include checking (cash), accounts receivable, inventory, and accounts payable. The Checking register in Figure 1.4 shows some of Rock Castle's cash payments and cash receipts, and provides cash balances after each transaction.

The financial effects of business transactions may be entered directly into the register or into the forms that automatically record the effects of these transactions in the relevant register. For example, if an owner's cash contribution is recorded on a Deposit form, the increases in both the checking account and relevant owner's equity account are simultaneously recorded in the Checking register and Contributed Capital register.

Reports and Graphs

QuickBooks **reports** and **graphs** present the financial position and the operating results of a company in a way that makes business decision

Figure 1.3

An Invoice Form for Rock Castle Construction

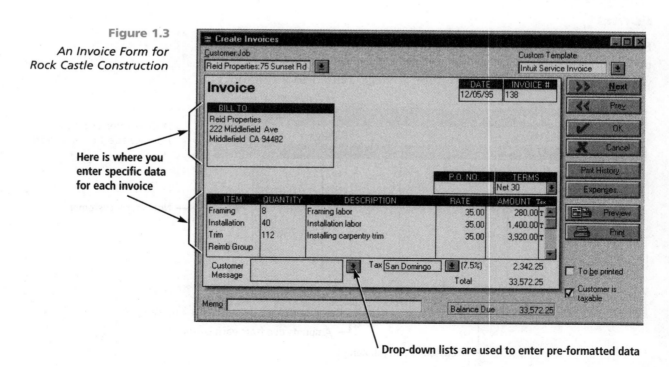

Here is where you enter specific data for each invoice

Drop-down lists are used to enter pre-formatted data

Cash payments   Cash receipts

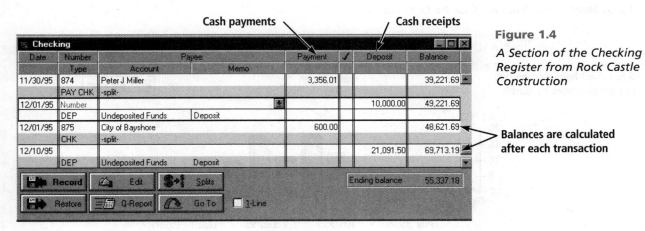

Figure 1.4

A Section of the Checking Register from Rock Castle Construction

Balances are calculated after each transaction

making easier. The Profit and Loss report in Figure 1.5 shows the revenues and expenses of Rock Castle Construction for a specific period of time. Note that QuickBooks uses the title "Profit and Loss," but the generally accepted accounting title for this report is "Income Statement." Titles for this and other reports are all changeable using QuickBooks's Header/Footer button. You can modify reports in many other ways, such as by comparing monthly periods, comparing this year with prior years, or examining year-to-date activity.

QuickBooks can also graph data to illustrate a company's financial position and operating results. For example, the bar chart in Figure 1.6 illustrates sales by month and the pie chart illustrates sales by construction category.

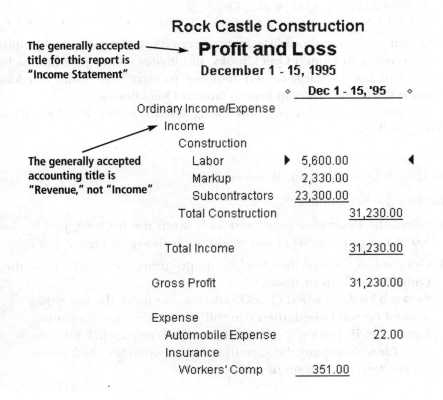

Figure 1.5

A Profit and Loss Report (Income Statement) from Rock Castle Construction

Figure 1.6 *A Sales Graph from Rock Castle Construction*

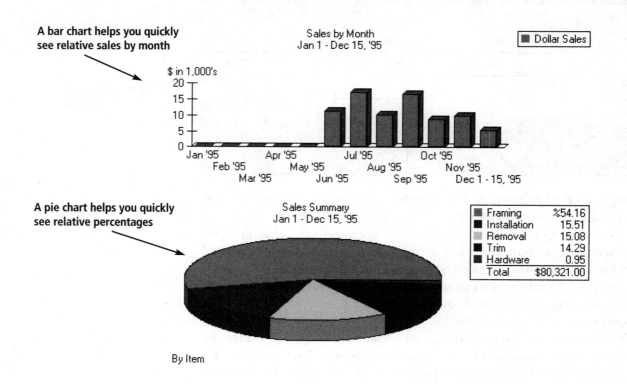

A bar chart helps you quickly see relative sales by month

A pie chart helps you quickly see relative percentages

LAUNCHING QUICKBOOKS

Now that you know about lists, forms, registers, and reports and graphs, you are ready to launch QuickBooks. Jim invites you to join him in his office and use his large-screen monitor to start your tour. You load Windows, and Jim tells you how to launch QuickBooks.

Follow the steps for your operating system, either Windows 95 or Windows 3.1.

To launch QuickBooks in Windows 95:

1 Click the **Start** button.

2 Select the **Programs** menu and look down the list for QuickBooks 5.0. An example of what you might see is shown in Figure 1.7.

3 Once you've located the QuickBooks program, click and release the **QuickBooks** icon or name.

trouble? If, when QuickBooks was last used, the file being worked on was closed, then you will see the message shown in Figure 1.8. If, however, a QuickBooks file is open, click **File**, then click **Close Company**. Be sure to close any open files before you proceed to the next set of steps.

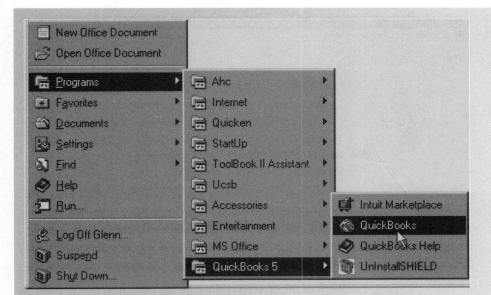

Figure 1.7

Launching QuickBooks in Windows 95

Figure 1.8

No Company File Open Message

or

To launch QuickBooks in Windows 3.1:

1 Look for an icon or window titled QuickBooks. See Figure 1.9.

2 If you see the QuickBooks group icon, double-click the **QuickBooks group** icon to open the group window. If you see the QuickBooks group window instead of the group icon, go to Step 3.

3 Double-click the **QuickBooks** icon. After a short pause, the QuickBooks opening screen appears.
trouble? If, when QuickBooks was last used, the file being worked on was closed, then you will see the message shown in Figure 1.8. If, however, a QuickBooks file is open, click **File**, then click **Close Company**. Be sure to close any open files before you proceed to the next set of steps.

Figure 1.9

Launching QuickBooks in Windows 3.1

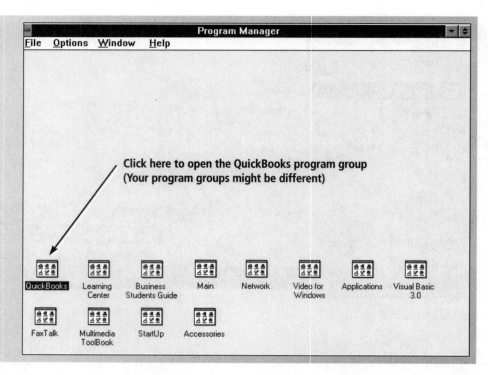

Now that you have launched QuickBooks, you can begin to learn how to use it.

OPENING A QUICKBOOKS FILE

Jim hands you a disk and tells you to open a file called rock.qbw. (You will find this file included on your Student Disks).

To open Rock Castle Construction Company's file:

1 Insert the Student Disk into your computer's disk drive.

2 Click **File**.

3 Click **Open Company**. The Open a Company window appears. If the A: drive icon is not displayed in the Drives box, as shown in Figure 1.10, click the **Down Arrow** button on the Drives box; then from the list of drives, click the **A:** drive icon. A list of available files on drive A: appears.

4 Click the **rock.qbw** file. See Figure 1.10.

5 Click the **OK** button in the Open a Company window.

6 The QuickBooks Information window appears, as shown in Figure 1.11. Your window might look slightly different. Note that rock.qbw is a modified version of QuickBooks's sample file, and it will assume a system date of December 15, 1997.

Click here after you select a file

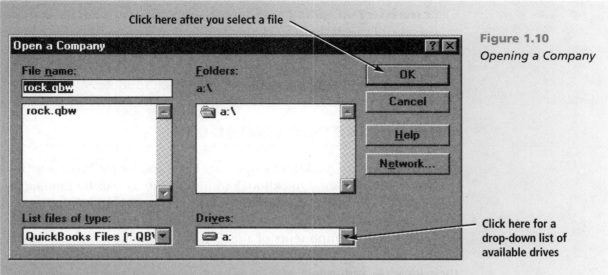

Figure 1.10
Opening a Company

Click here for a
drop-down list of
available drives

Figure 1.11
QuickBooks Information Window

trouble? If your floppy disk drive is B or is identified by some other letter, substitute the correct letter in this and all future steps whenever you are instructed to work with drive A.

7 Click the **OK** button. The Inside Tips window appears. Let's skip this useful tool for now and click **Done**. The QuickBooks Reminders window appears. See Figure 1.12. QuickBooks automatically opens the Reminders window every time you open a file, unless you change a default setting. You will learn how to change this setting later. For now, close this window.

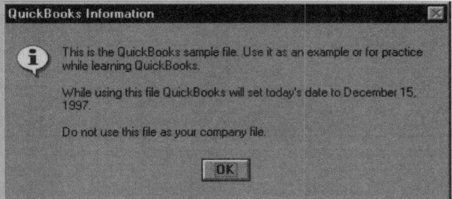

Figure 1.12
The Reminders Window

trouble? If your QuickBooks Application window does not already fill the desktop, click the **Application window Maximize button**, located next to the Close button (*Windows 3.1 Note:* You can maximize windows in Windows 3.1 by clicking on the maximize button located in the upper-right corner of each window.)

THE QUICKBOOKS WINDOW

Jim explains that QuickBooks operates like most other Windows programs, so most of the QuickBooks window controls will be familiar to you if you have used other Windows programs. He reaches for the mouse and quickly clicks a few times until his screen looks like Figure 1.13. The main components of the QuickBooks window are shown in this figure. Let's take a look at these components so you are familiar with their location and use.

The **title bar** at the top of the window tells you that you are in the QuickBooks program and identifies the company file currently open. The **menu bar** contains the **command menus**, which open windows within QuickBooks. The File, Edit, and Help menus are similar to other Windows programs in that they allow you to perform such common tasks as open, save, copy, paste, find, and get help.

The Lists menu gives you access to all lists, including the chart of accounts, customers, vendors, employees, and inventory items, to name a few. The Activities menu contains commands to create invoices, receive payments, make deposits, write checks, enter bills, and so on. The Reports and Graphs menus generate financial statements, schedules, or graphs, all of which can be customized to fit your needs.

Figure 1.13
Components of the QuickBooks Window

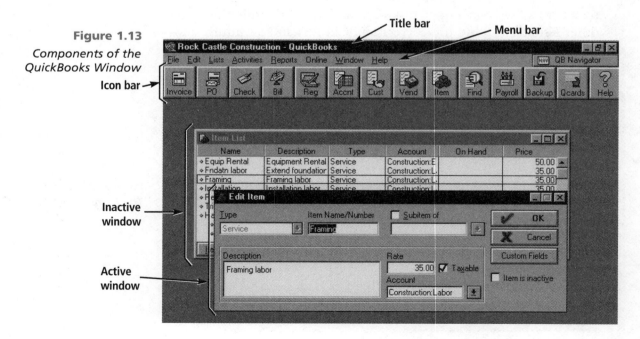

The **icon bar** contains some of the most commonly used menu commands. The QuickBooks default icon bar, shown in Figure 1.13, starts activities such as creating invoices and purchase orders, writing checks, entering bills, and paying employees. Additional icons open lists such as the chart of accounts, customers, vendors, or items. When you are more familiar with QuickBooks, you might want to modify the icon bar to include those activities you perform most often.

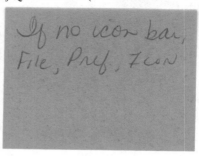

If no icon bar, File, Pref, Icon

The **active window** is the window in which you can enter or edit data, and it is identified by a solid window title bar. Only one window may be active at a time. Other windows may be open, but they are inactive. If the active window is closed, or if a window behind it is selected, it becomes **inactive**, and the window selected becomes active.

dark blue

SAVING AND CLOSING
A QUICKBOOKS FILE
. . . .

Now that you have seen the components of the QuickBooks screen, Jim wants to show you how to close a file, so that you will always be able to save your work and exit QuickBooks. He explains that to close a QuickBooks file, you can do one of three things:

- Exit QuickBooks using the Exit command on the File menu.
- Open another company file using the Open Company command.
- Close the file using the Close Company command on the File menu.

To close the Rock Castle Construction Company's file:

1 Click **File**.

2 Click **Exit**. The Rock Castle Construction Company file is automatically saved and closed. A dialog box might display the message "Intuit highly recommends backing up your data to avoid any accidental loss. Would you like to back up now?" Another message about Quickbooks Update Service might also appear. Close this message window for now.

3 Click **No** to exit QuickBooks and return to Windows.

And then Jim tells you something very unusual. He says that unlike other Windows programs, QuickBooks *does not have a Save command.* In other words, in QuickBooks you cannot save a file whenever you want. You stare at Jim in disbelief and ask how that can be possible. Jim explains that *QuickBooks automatically saves all of the data you input and changes you make as soon as you make them and click OK.* Jim admits that when he first used QuickBooks, he was uneasy about exiting the program until he could find a way to save his work. But he discovered that there are no Save or Save As commands on the QuickBooks File menu as there are on most other Windows programs. He reassures you that as unsettling as this is, you'll get used to it when you become more familiar with QuickBooks.

CORRECTING MISTAKES: THE BACKSPACE KEY, THE UNDO COMMAND, AND THE REVERT COMMAND

Another skill you must have when you start using a program that's new to you is how to correct mistakes. Jim explains that, as with many other programs, one of the easiest ways to correct a mistake while entering data into QuickBooks is to use the Backspace key. Whenever you are typing and need to correct a mistake, you can press the Backspace key to back up the cursor and delete one or more characters. To demonstrate this error correction method, let's use rock.qbw again and intentionally make a mistake when entering a cash sale.

To correct a mistake as you are typing:

1 Open rock.qbw as you have done before.

2 Click **Activities**, then click **Enter Cash Sales**. The Enter Cash Sales window appears.

3 Move the cursor to the SOLD TO field. Type **United Ari** in the SOLD TO field to make the intentional error, as shown in Figure 1.14, *but don't press [Enter].*

Figure 1.14

Correcting Mistakes Using the Backspace Key

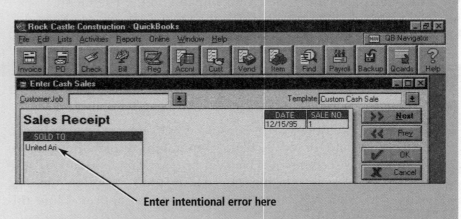

Enter intentional error here

4 Press [**Backspace**] twice to delete the "ri".

5 Type **irlines** and press [**Enter**] to make the correction.

The correct customer name is now entered in the SOLD TO field of the Cash Sales form, and the cursor is positioned to enter the customer's address.

Two other useful ways to correct mistakes are to use the Undo command and the Revert command. Both of these are located on the Edit menu. The Undo command is so called because it "undoes" all typing since the last Enter command. The Revert command causes the form to revert back to the form's initial appearance. To demonstrate how to use these commands, let's continue filling in the form for Sample Company and enter an address for United Airlines.

To correct a mistake after typing several words:

1 Type **10000 Skyway Blvd.** under United Airlines in the SOLD TO field, *but don't press [Enter]*. You think that this is the correct address for United Airlines.

2 You then discover that this is not the correct address. Click **Edit**, then click **Undo Typing** to delete the entire address. See Figure 1.15.

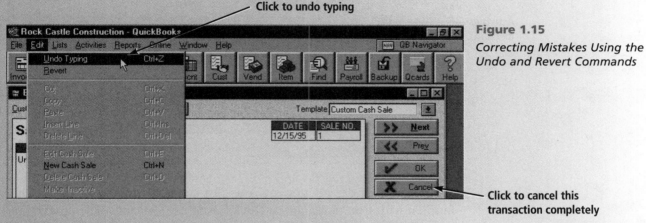

Figure 1.15

Correcting Mistakes Using the Undo and Revert Commands

3 Type **1234 Airline Way**, the correct address, and press **[Enter]**.

4 Type **Chicago, Illinois 30021** and press **[Enter]**.

5 Now suppose that the United Airlines purchasing agent changes her mind, and you don't have a reason to enter this cash sale at all. Click **Edit**, then click **Revert**. The form returns or "reverts" to its original appearance.

6 Let's completely cancel this transaction. Click the **Cancel** button to leave this form without entering the cash sale into the Sample Company's accounts.

QUICKBOOKS'S MENU COMMANDS

Jim explains that to enter cash sales, create invoices, pay bills, receive payments, and so on, you use QuickBooks menu commands. Some of these functions are also available from buttons on the QuickBooks button bar.

Some QuickBooks menus are dynamic; in other words the options on the menu change depending upon what form, list, register, or report you are working with. For instance, when you enter cash sales information, the File and Edit menus change to include menu commands to print the cash sale, or to edit, delete, memorize, or void the cash sale.

The menu that you will use perhaps the most is the Activities menu. You use this menu every time you want to enter data into QuickBooks. Figure 1.16 displays all of the commands on the Activities menu. This menu is also dynamic.

Figure 1.16
The Activities Menu

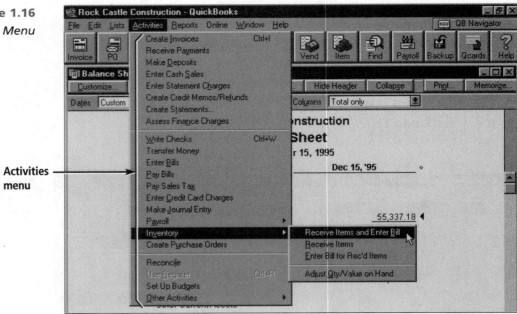

Activities
menu

Because this is all new to you, Jim suggests that first you become familiar with how managers at Rock Castle use QuickBooks to make business decisions.

USING QUICKBOOKS TO MAKE BUSINESS DECISIONS: AN EXAMPLE AT ROCK CASTLE

Once transactions are entered into the QuickBooks accounting information system, they can be accessed, revised, organized, and reported in many ways to aid business decision making. This ability is what makes a computerized accounting information system so valuable to managers.

While you're sitting with Jim, he receives a phone call from Susan Guttmann, the manager of Rock Castle Construction's credit department. Susan needs some information to help her decide if any past due accounts should be turned over to a collection agency. You know from your accounting course that Susan is really asking for information about Rock Castle's **accounts receivable**, or amounts due from customers from previously recorded sales. Susan wants to know how much is due from customers and how current those receivables are; specifically, which customers owe Rock Castle and when their payments were due. Jim tells Susan he'll look into this immediately and call her right back.

To identify the customers who owe Rock Castle money and the total amount of receivables due from these customers:

1 Click **Reports**, click **A/R Reports**, and then click **Aging Detail**. Notice the difference between the report on your screen and Figure 1.17. Specifically, note the date beneath the title "A/R Aging

Detail." The year 1997 is on your screen, but 1995 is in the title of the report. It is *essential* that you now learn exactly why this difference occurs here and throughout Chapter 1. The reason is that the events described in the Rock Castle Construction case occurred in 1995. Quickbooks 5.0 (for Rock Castle only), however, uses the computer system date of December 15, 1997. To reconcile this difference and to help you work with the 1995 case material, *you must change the date on your screen* so that you are looking at 1995 data for Rock Castle, rather than 1997 data.

**Purchase order column resized to view
the entire width of the report**

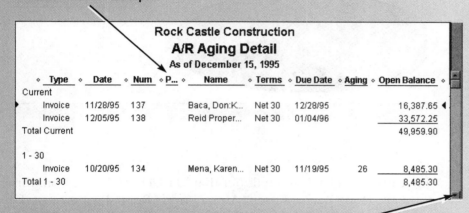

Figure 1.17
Accounts Receivable Detail

Scroll down to view additional information

trouble? The report you see might be slightly different from the one shown in Figure 1.17. Some column widths have been altered. Use the scroll bars to view this report both vertically and horizontally.

2 Move the cursor into the Dates box directly above the title of the report. Change "97" to "95". Then with your cursor on the report, click once. Your screen will be refreshed and look like Figure 1.17. Be sure to scroll your window up to the top to see the start of the data. When you view the Rock Castle Construction case, you might need to make this change. To help you know when to make this change, you will see the **CHANGE DATE** symbol.

CHANGE DATE

3 Scroll down this summary report, and note that three customers owe Rock Castle a total of $118,445.20.

4 Jim wants to see a graphic illustration of this information. Click **Reports**, then click **Graphs**, and finally click **Accounts Receivable**. Once again, change the date from 1997 to 1995. The graphic in Figure 1.18 appears.

CHANGE DATE

Figure 1.18

Accounts Receivable by Aging Period and Customer

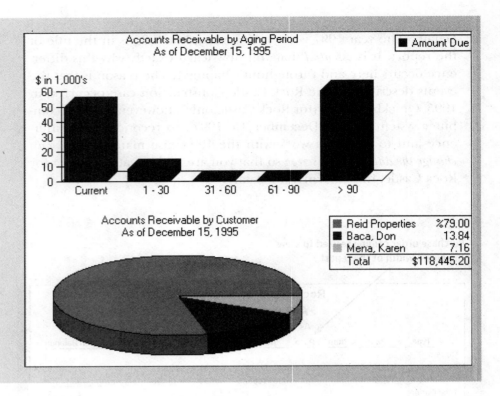

Jim calls Susan back and tells her that $118,445.20 is due from three customers: Don Baca, Karen Mena, and Reid Properties. The $49,959.90 due from Baca and Reid is current, while $8,485.30 due from Mena and $60,000.00 due from Reid are past due. Susan says that only Mena concerns her as she's already working on the Reid past due amount. She'd like to know specifically when invoices were sent to Mena, when Mena made payments, and in what amounts. Jim knows he can easily get this information by accessing the Customer Balance Detail for Mena.

To access the Customer Balance Detail for Mena:

1 Click **Reports**, click **A/R Reports**, then click **Customer Balance Detail**.

2 Scroll down the report to **Karen Mena's** detailed information shown in Figure 1.19. This report describes the two invoices that billed Karen Mena for construction services rendered. It also shows the cash payments received to date from Mena.

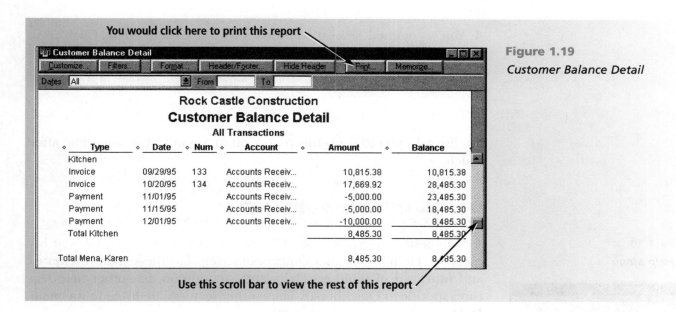

Figure 1.19
Customer Balance Detail

Jim calls Susan back and tells her that the invoice dates are 9/29/95 and 10/20/95, and that the dates of the most recent payments are 11/01/95, 11/15/95, and 12/01/95. He has quickly and easily accessed financial information from the company's QuickBooks data file and Susan thanks him. She is grateful for his quick response so she can make her decision. She asks if, before the end of the day, he would print out a copy of this information and leave it on her desk. Jim is happy to oblige.

PRINTING IN QUICKBOOKS

Jim suddenly remembers a meeting he must attend. But before exiting QuickBooks you remind him that he promised to print a Customer Balance Summary report for Susan.

To print a Customer Balance Summary report:

1 Click **Reports**, click **A/R Reports**, then click **Customer Balance Summary**.

2 Click the **Print** button located on the right side of the button bar. See Figure 1.19.

3 Click **Print** in the Print Report dialog box. The report prints out. **trouble?** You might have to set up a printer before printing. If necessary, click **Cancel** in the Print Report dialog box. Then select **Printer Setup** from the **File** menu. QuickBooks allows you to set up different printers for different functions. Click the **Settings** tab and select the printer you would like to use from the Printer name drop-down list.

4 You've opened several windows and not closed them. Click the **Windows** menu, and then click **Close All** to close all open windows and return to the QuickBooks opening window.

Jim asks you to drop this report off at Susan's desk sometime after lunch.

USING QUICKBOOKS HELP

Figure 1.20

The Help Menu

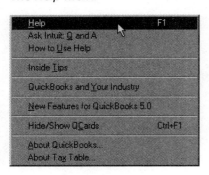

Jim suggests you explore QuickBooks' Help features while he is at his meeting. He tells you that QuickBooks Help has the standard features and functions of Windows Help, and, in addition, has other help features specific to QuickBooks. These other features are listed in the main Help menu shown in Figure 1.20.

As with other Windows programs, you can access Help by clicking on the green text. QuickBooks Help is context sensitive—that is, different help screens appear depending on where you are in the program. You can get help for a specific topic by using the Search feature of Help.

You decide to follow up on Jim's suggestion to look at a help feature he finds very useful, the **Overviews**—flowcharts that graphically show how QuickBooks handles some of the major accounting processes and cycles.

To view the Sales Overview:

1 Click **Help** from the menu bar. Then click **Help** on the menu. (Alternatively, as with other Windows programs, you could press F1 from anywhere in QuickBooks.)

2 Click the **Contents** tab, then double-click on **A quick look at Quickbooks**. See Figure 1.21 (on the following page).

3 Double-click **Sales**. Figure 1.22 appears.

4 Scroll down this window to view the process of recording a sale and collecting payment.

5 Close this window.

You will have an opportunity to use most of these options in this and later chapters.

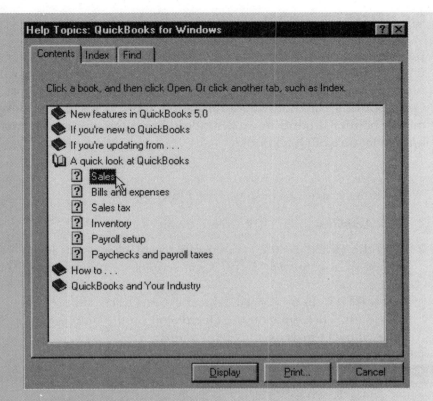

Figure 1.21
Help Topics

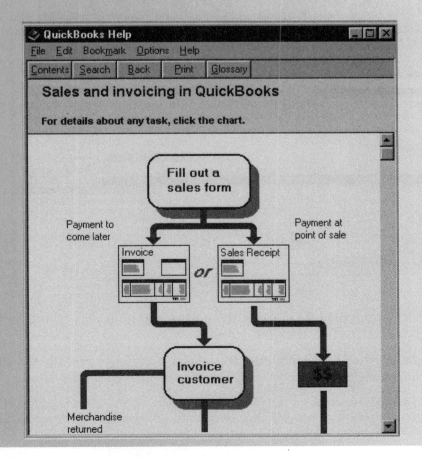

Figure 1.22
Overview for Sales and Invoicing

QCARDS

Jim returns from his meeting. He asks if you've discovered Qcards. He finds all of these QuickBooks features very useful, but he particularly recommends that you use the Qcards feature as you begin to work with QuickBooks. Qcards provide information about fields as you move the mouse pointer around in each window. Jim offers to demonstrate this unique feature of QuickBooks.

To see how Qcards can help you use QuickBooks:

1 Click **Activities**, then click **Create Invoices**.

2 Read the Qcard for the create invoice activity, which is located in a corner of the invoice form. Your screen should look similar to Figure 1.23.

   trouble? If no Qcard appears, the Qcard feature might be turned off. Click once on the **Qcard** icon on the button bar, or click **Hide/Show Qcards** on the Help menu.

Figure 1.23

Qcards as a Help Feature

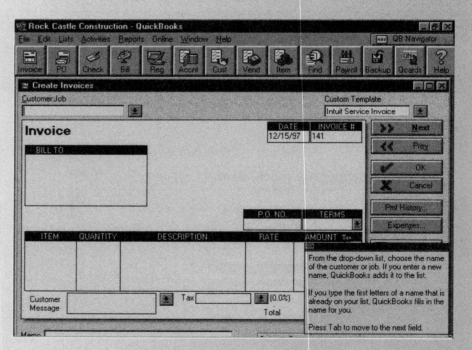

3 Click in the **BILL TO** field of the invoice and notice how the Qcard changes.

4 Click in the **ITEM** column of the invoice and notice how the Qcard changes again.

5 Close this window.

Qcards are available for all lists, forms, registers, and reports. You might find them helpful when you first learn to use QuickBooks, but eventually you might want to turn them off. As you saw in the **trouble?** section for Step 2 in the last set of steps, you can turn Qcards on and off by using either the Qcard icon on the button bar or the Hide/Show Qcards menu item on the Help menu. You can also use the Preferences menu.

QUICKBOOKS SMALL BUSINESS ONLINE SERVICE

QuickBooks 5.0 has an online feature which, if your computer has Internet access, you might find helpful. Jim's computer is currently connected to the Internet via a company-wide network that uses the popular Netscape Navigator as its World Wide Web browser.

Jim offers to demonstrate the Small Business Online (SBO) service to you.

To access the Small Business Online service:

1 Click **Online** from the main menu bar, click **Intuit Web Sites**, then click **QuickBooks Small Business Online**. After some time, a QuickBooks home page will appear. See Figure 1.24.

   trouble? Your computer might require access codes for entering the Internet. Check with your system administrator or lab coordinator.

   trouble? If you have never connected to the Internet using Quickbooks, you will need to follow the onscreen directions to go through the Internet Connection Setup.

Figure 1.24
QuickBooks Small Business Online Home Page

   trouble? If you do not have access to the Internet on your computer, skip these steps and go to "Exiting QuickBooks."

   trouble? Home pages are always changing, so your screen might be different and still be the QuickBooks SBO home page.

2 Scroll down this page. Several feature articles are available for review. Pick an article that interests you most. Click on the article and review its content.

3 Close the browser window, and return to QuickBooks.

THE QUICKBOOKS NAVIGATOR

Besides Qcards, Jim explains, there is a feature new to Version 5.0—QuickBooks Navigator—that you might find useful. He tells you to think of it as your starting point to find lists, forms, registers, or reports. As you saw earlier, when you launch QuickBooks, the QuickBooks Navigator appears in the center of the main QuickBooks window. If you choose to hide it, a QB Navigator button appears in the upper-right corner of the QuickBooks window, and you can redisplay it at any time by clicking this button.

To view QuickBooks Navigator:

1 Be sure that no companies are open, then open rock.qbw as you have done before. Close the Tips and Reminders windows, but do not close the Navigator window.

2 Notice the tabs down the left side of the Navigator window. There are usually six tabs here, each for a different area of the QuickBooks program. Each tab helps you find the task you want to do. Click the **Purchases and Vendors** tab and notice how the central part of the Navigator window changes.

3 Most tabs contain a flowchart that shows the activities of this tab. Double-click the **Purchase Orders** icon. A purchase order form appears. Close this window.

4 Below the flowchart are reports that provide information relevant to this tab. Click some of the report titles listed, and then close those report windows.

After you have learned the basics about QuickBooks in this course, you might decide to use the QuickBooks Navigator. But for now, follow the steps as they are written in this text.

EXITING QUICKBOOKS

You thank Jim for taking the time to introduce you to QuickBooks as he rushes off to yet another meeting. You know you can probably exit QuickBooks on your own, using standard Windows commands. You choose to use the Exit command on the File menu.

To exit QuickBooks:

1 Click **File** on the QuickBooks menu bar to display the File menu.

2 Click **Exit**. Once again a dialog box might display the message "Intuit highly recommends backing up your data to avoid any accidental loss. Would you like to back up now?" See Figure 1.25.

3 Click **No** to exit QuickBooks and return to Windows. Good accounting practice encourages backing up data files, but backup is not necessary now with these sample files.

Figure 1.25
Automatic Backup

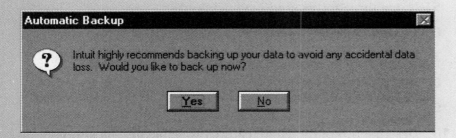

END NOTE

Jim has shown you some of the features of QuickBooks 5.0, how to navigate these features, and how business decisions can be aided by the reporting and analysis of accounting information afforded by QuickBooks. You are impressed by the speed at which information is made available and are anxious to learn more.

practice

Session 1 Questions

1 Describe, in your own words, the various uses of QuickBooks.

2 List the four basic features of QuickBooks.

3 Describe how lists are used in QuickBooks.

4 Describe how forms are used in QuickBooks.

5 Name three forms used in QuickBooks.

6 Describe how registers are used in QuickBooks.

7 Describe how reports and graphs are used in QuickBooks.

8 Describe the function of the Activities menu.

9 Describe how to print a report in QuickBooks.

10 Describe two of the Help features available in QuickBooks.

Session 1 Assignments

1 *Working with Files: Opening, Closing, and Printing*

Use the Rock Castle Construction Company file to practice opening, closing, and printing.

 a. Open the rock.qbw file from your Student Disk in drive A:.

 b. Create a report of Open Invoices from the A/R Reports menu item on the Reports menu. Be sure the date 12/15/95 is specified.

 CHANGE DATE

 c. Print the Open Invoices report.

2 *Practice Using the QuickBooks Help Menu*

Use the QuickBooks Help menu to learn more about QuickBooks's features.

 a. From the Help menu, select **Help**. Then open the Contents section of QuickBooks Help. Next open **A quick look at QuickBooks**. View each of the overview topics listed and print a copy of one.

 b. Open the Index section of QuickBooks Help to learn more about customer type lists. Print the screen displayed.

 c. From the "How to" section of the Contents menu choose the **Accounts and taxes** section, and then select **Your chart of accounts.** Select the appropriate options to learn how to add a new account. Describe, in your own words, the process of adding a new account.

d. Select **Glossary** from the Help menu. Define the following terms in one sentence each:

Accounts Receivable	Chart of Accounts
Assets	Equity
Balance Sheet	Liabilities

3 *Using the QuickBooks Small Business Online Service*

a. If you have Internet access, select **Intuit Web Sites** from the **Online** menu. Then select **QuickBooks Small Business Online.**

trouble? If your computer connection doesn't automatically connect to Intuit you may need to enter the following address in your Internet browser: **http://www.intuit.com/ quickbooks/.**

Information about QuickBooks software can be found at **http://www.intuit.com/ quickbooks/**

http://

b. View the Support Services section.

c. Summarize the information available in this section.

4 *Using the South-Western Home Page for More Assignments or Cases*

If you have Internet access, go to the home page for this textbook at **owen.swcollege.com**.

Click **Additional Problems Sets**, and then select the **Chapter 1: Session 1** section, and complete the problem(s) your instructor assigns.

Go to **owen.swcollege.com**

http://

5 *Using the QuickBooks Technical Support Service*

a. If you have Internet access, choose **Internet Web Sites** from the **Online** menu. Then select **QuickBooks Technical Support.**

trouble? If your computer connection doesn't automatically connect to Intuit, you may need to enter the following address in your Internet browser: **http://www.intuit.com/ quickbooks/technical_support.**

Support for QuickBooks software can be found at **http://www.intuit.com/**

http://

b. Identify one of the top ten most asked questions listed in this section.

Session 1 Case Problems: Rock Castle Construction Company

1 *Accessing Inventory Data*

Jim Reed, Rock Castle's accountant, wants to know the amount and nature of inventory on hand as of December 15, 1995. Use rock.qbw to obtain this inventory information. Write your responses to Questions *c* through *e,* and print the Inventory Valuation Summary report.

a. Open rock.qbw.
b. Open an Inventory Valuation Summary report as of December 15, 1995.
c. What items of inventory were on hand on that date?
d. How many of each item were on hand on that date?
e. What was the average cost of those items on that date?
f. Print the Inventory Valuation Summary report.

2 *Accessing Sales Data*

Jim Reed, Rock Castle's accountant, wants to know the company's sales for the period December 1 through December 15, 1995. Use rock.qbw to obtain this sales information. Write your responses to Questions *c* through *f,* and print the Sales by Customer Detail report.

a. Open rock.qbw.
b. Open the Sales by Customer Detail report for the period December 1 through December 15, 1995.
c. What customer was billed in this period?
d. What items are included on this invoice?
e. At what rate per hour was this customer billed?
f. What is the total amount of this invoice?
g. Print the Sales by Customer Detail report.

Preparing a Balance Sheet Using QuickBooks

Learning Objectives

In this session you will:

- Create a comparative balance sheet and a summary balance sheet
- Investigate detail supporting balance sheet items
- Use the Balance Sheet Report button bar
- Create a balance sheet as of a specific date other than the system date
- Print a balance sheet

CASE: ROCK CASTLE CONSTRUCTION COMPANY

It's your second day at your new job, and you arrive early. Jim is already hard at work at the computer. He tells you he is preparing for Rock Castle's fiscal year-end on December 31, 1995. Since this is the first time he will prepare financial statements using QuickBooks, he's a little nervous. So he's decided to practice for the year-end closing by preparing a preliminary balance sheet as of December 15, 1995.

You recall from your accounting course that a balance sheet reports the assets, liabilities, and owners' equity of a company at a specific point in time. As part of your continued training on QuickBooks, Jim asks you to watch what he does as he prepares the preliminary balance sheet. He explains that his immediate goals are to familiarize himself with how to prepare a balance sheet using QuickBooks, and to examine some of the valuable features QuickBooks provides to help managers analyze and interpret financial information.

CREATING A BALANCE SHEET

You know from your business courses that the information on a balance sheet can be presented in many ways. Jim tells you that QuickBooks provides four preset ways to present a balance sheet; QuickBooks also allows him to customize the way he presents the information. He decides to examine one of the preset balance sheets first. He chooses what QuickBooks calls the Standard Balance Sheet report.

To create a Standard Balance Sheet report:

1 Launch QuickBooks and then open rock.qbw from your Student Disk in drive A:.

CHANGE DATE

2 Click **Reports**, click **Balance Sheet**, then click **Standard**. Change the As of date to 12/15/95 and click once. QuickBooks's Standard Balance Sheet appears. See Figure 1.26.

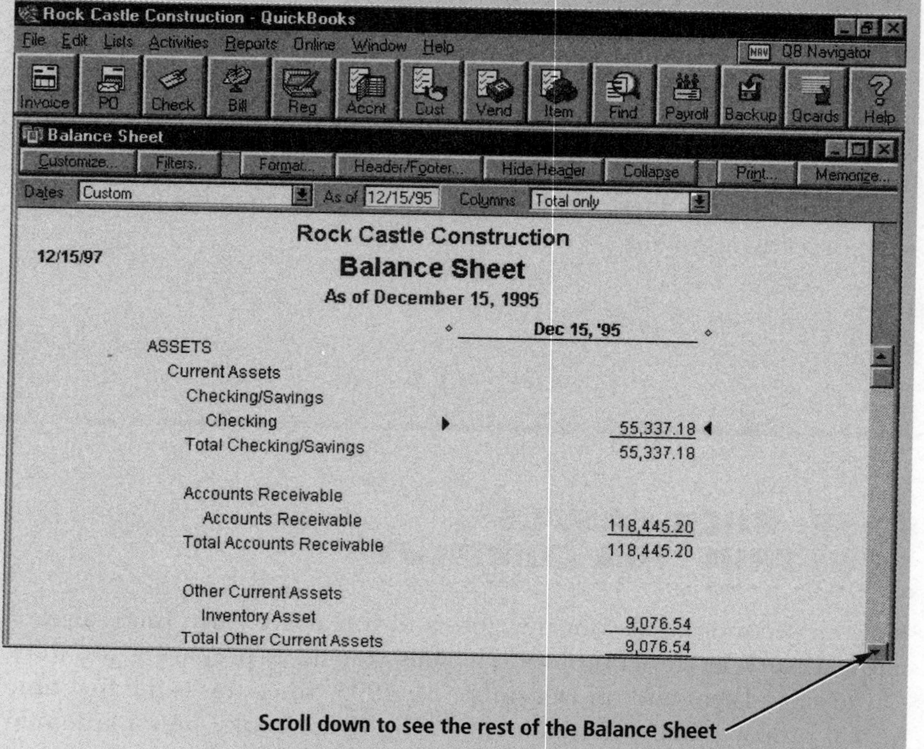

Figure 1.26

Rock Castle's Balance Sheet as of December 15, 1995 in QuickBooks's Standard Preset Report

Scroll down to see the rest of the Balance Sheet

3 Scroll down the Rock Castle Construction Company Balance Sheet. Notice that this report shows the balance in each account, with subtotals for assets, liabilities, and owners' equity. Unlike standard accounting practice, QuickBooks displays net income for the year-to-date as part of owners' equity. In particular, take note of the current assets, fixed assets, current liabilities, long-term liabilities, and owners' equity. Note that QuickBooks refers to "owners' equity" as simply "equity."

4 Close this window.

Jim is amazed at how rapidly QuickBooks created this balance sheet compared to how long it's taken him to create one manually in the past. As you both look over this balance sheet, Jim comments that because he generated this information so quickly with so little effort, he might now be able to add information to balance sheets that he didn't have time to include before. For example, he has always wanted to include comparative information on balance sheets to help Rock Castle's managers make better business decisions.

CREATING A COMPARATIVE BALANCE SHEET

By using the search function of QuickBooks Help, Jim discovers that QuickBooks has a built-in feature for preparing comparative balance sheets. He learns from Help that as long as the comparative information has already been entered in the QuickBooks file, he can easily create a comparative balance sheet. He tells you he entered the opening balances and transactions from December 15, 1994. When he sees how easily he can create a comparative balance sheet, he decides to create one comparing the balance sheet of December 15, 1995 with the one of December 15, 1994.

To create a Comparative Balance Sheet report:

1 Click **Reports**, click **Balance Sheet**, and then click **Comparison**. Change the As of date to 12/15/95. Note that the standard accounting term is "comparative" balance sheet, not "comparison." Figure 1.27 appears.

CHANGE DATE

Drag to adjust column widths

Note the significance of these two columns

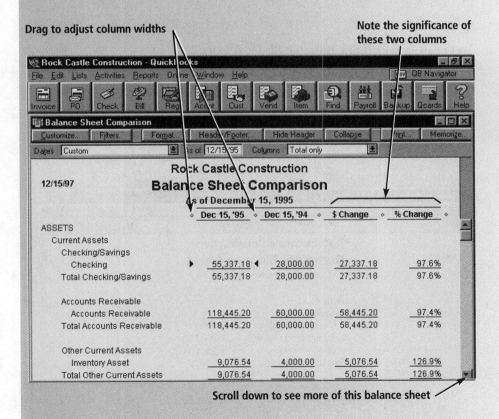

Figure 1.27

QuickBooks's Comparison Balance Sheet Report for Rock Castle as of December 15, 1995 and December 15, 1994

Scroll down to see more of this balance sheet

2 Scroll down and across this balance sheet. Note that this report is similar to the Standard report, except that the columns compare the amounts for this year-to-date and last year-to-date, and show the change in dollar amount and percent.

trouble? The balance sheet on your screen might not be the same as Figure 1.27, because the column widths are different. To change the column widths on any QuickBooks report, click and hold the mouse over the small diamond-shaped symbols to the right or left of any column. Drag to the right or left to increase or decrease each column's width. A dialog box might appear asking if you want to make all columns the same width. You may answer yes or no.

3 Close this window.

CREATING A SUMMARY BALANCE SHEET

Jim wonders if QuickBooks has a preset report that summarizes balance sheet information—in other words one that provides no detail, only totals. In annual reports, such a summary is useful to external financial statement users, who usually do not have much interest in detailed balance sheet information. Jim again consults Help and learns that QuickBooks has a Summary Balance Sheet preset report.

To create a Summary Balance Sheet report:

1 Click **Reports**, click **Balance Sheet**, and then click **Summary**. Change the As of date to 12/15/95 and click once. See Figure 1.28.

CHANGE DATE

Figure 1.28
QuickBooks's Summary Balance Sheet Report for Rock Castle

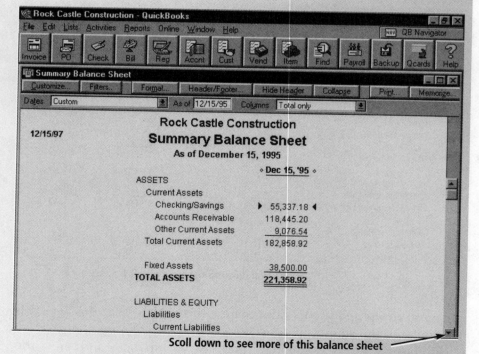

Scoll down to see more of this balance sheet

2 Scroll down the Summary Balance Sheet. Note that it is a brief version of the Standard Balance Sheet; it shows amounts for each account type, such as Other Current Assets, but not for individual accounts within each account type.

INVESTIGATING THE BALANCE SHEET USING QUICKZOOM

Now that Jim knows he can generate the type of reports he wants, he decides to investigate QuickZoom—a feature he has heard QuickBooks provides for most reports. He tells you that QuickZoom shows you what transaction or transactions underlie any amount found in a report. You know that this is a helpful feature because managers often need to be able to quickly explain report balances; thus, knowledge of the underlying detailed transactions is essential.

Jim decides to practice using QuickZoom by analyzing the transactions that make up the Accounts Receivable balance.

To use QuickZoom:

1 Click the Accounts Receivable balance of **118,445.20**. A cursor shaped like a magnifying glass and containing a "Z" appears. This cursor indicates that a QuickZoom report is available for this amount. See Figure 1.29.

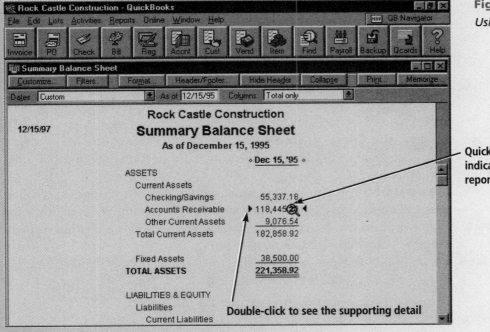

Figure 1.29
Using QuickZoom

QuickZoom cursor indicates a QuickZoom report is available

CHANGE DATE

2 Double-click the amount **118,445.20**. Change the From date to 1/1/95 and the To date to 12/15/95. Then click once. A transaction detail report, called Transactions by Account, appears. See Figure 1.30. The items listed in the Type column of this report—invoices and payments (that is, collections from customers)—represent the transactions that increased or decreased Accounts Receivable during the period from 1/01/95 to 12/15/95.

Figure 1.30

Viewing Transactions by Account

Transactions are listed for 1/1/95 through 12/15/95

Transactions are listed in date order

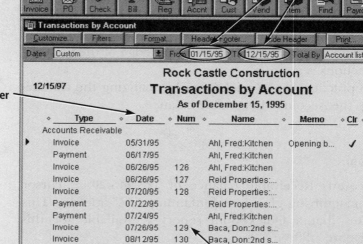

Double-click here to view Invoice 129

Double-click here to view payment received

3 Double-click **129** in the Num column to examine one of the actual invoices. Invoice number 129 appears. See Figure 1.31. This invoice to Don Baca for a total of $31,568.25 is dated 7/26/95.

4 Close the Create Invoices window. The Transactions by Account report, which was hidden while you examined Invoice number 129, reappears.

trouble? If the transactions report does not reappear, activate the Transactions by Account report by clicking Transactions by Account on the Window menu; or, if you closed the window, repeat Steps 1 through 4 above as necessary.

5 Double-click anywhere on the row containing the payment made by Don Baca posted 8/25/95. A Receive Payments window appears. See Figure 1.32. Note that this payment is for Invoice 129.

6 Close the Receive Payments window.

7 Close the Transactions by Account window.

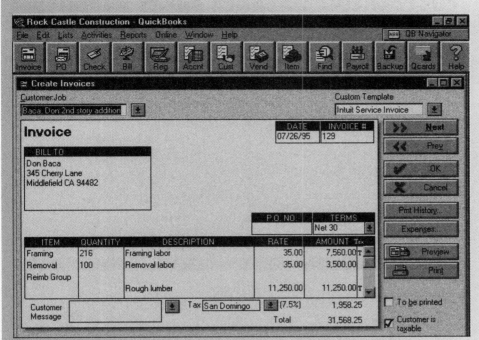

Figure 1.31

Examining Invoice Number 129 for Don Baca

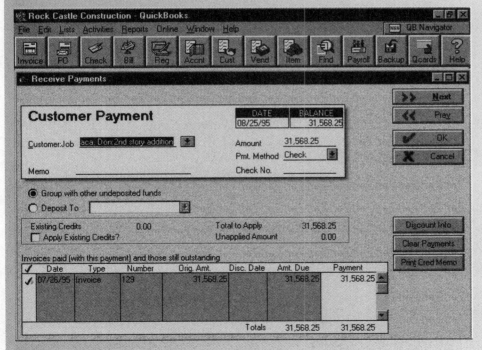

Figure 1.32

Customer Payment Received from Don Baca

Jim is pleased with the QuickZoom feature of QuickBooks because it allows him to quickly and easily investigate any of the balances reported.

CUSTOMIZING BALANCE SHEET REPORTS

The Balance Sheet report, like all other reports created in QuickBooks, can be customized using the Report button bar, located under the icon bar. Jim decides that since this comparative balance sheet is for internal use, he wants to change the heading, include the previous year's balances, report the numbers in thousands, and make a few other appropriate cosmetic changes.

To customize the Balance Sheet report:

1 Click the **Customize** button on the Report button bar.

2 Click the **Previous Year** check box as shown in Figure 1.33 to display the previous year's figures on the balance sheet.

Figure 1.33
The Customize Report Dialog Box

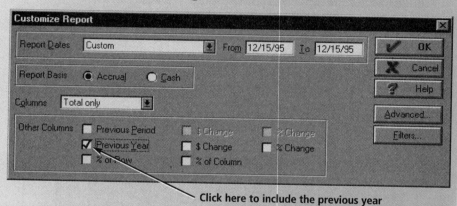

Click here to include the previous year

3 Click **OK**.

4 Click the **Format** button on the Report button bar.

5 Click the **Divided By 1000** and **Without Cents** check boxes under the Show All Numbers section of the Format Report dialog box. See Figure 1.34.

Figure 1.34
The Format Report Dialog Box

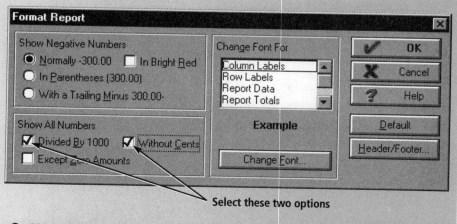

Select these two options

6 Click **OK**.

7 Click the **Header/Footer** button on the Report button bar.

8 Click inside the Report Title edit box. Change the name of the report from Summary Balance Sheet to Preliminary Balance Sheet by deleting the word "Summary" and typing **Preliminary** as shown in Figure 1.35.

Change the name of the report title

Select Left to left-align the title

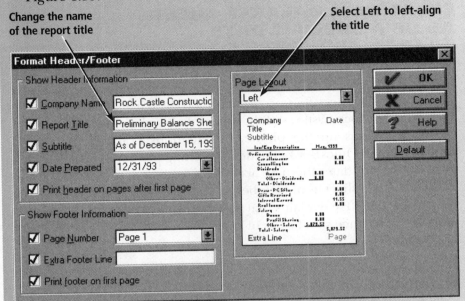

Figure 1.35
The Format Header/Footer Window

9 Change the page layout by clicking the **Down Arrow** in the Page Layout section and clicking **Left**. This changes the alignment of the title text to a left alignment.

10 Click **OK**. Figure 1.36 appears.

Comparative date for 1994 is now displayed

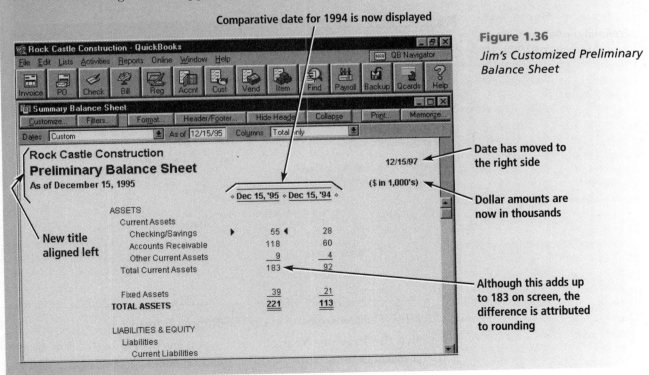

Figure 1.36
Jim's Customized Preliminary Balance Sheet

Date has moved to the right side

Dollar amounts are now in thousands

New title aligned left

Although this adds up to 183 on screen, the difference is attributed to rounding

Jim knows that this customized balance sheet will help Rock Castle's managers analyze the financial information more easily and quickly. You will have an opportunity to explore other report customization features available in QuickBooks in the Chapter Assignments.

CREATING A BALANCE SHEET AS OF A SPECIFIC DATE

Jim receives a phone call from Francis Wu, an accountant with Rock Castle's CPA firm of Stoddard & Wong. Francis says that she's trying to determine Rock Castle's allowance for uncollectibles and she'd like Jim to fax her a balance sheet for Rock Castle as of the end of the third quarter 1995.

As Jim hangs up the phone, he mentions Francis's request. He explains that in QuickBooks the default setting produces a balance sheet as of the system date, the date according to the computer. But Francis wants a balance sheet as of October 31, 1995. You ask Jim how to change the default date. He explains that you do this by specifying the date you want in the balance sheet's "As of" field.

To modify the Preliminary Balance Sheet report:

1 Click the **As of** box, which appears directly below the Header/Footer button. Delete 12/15 and type **10/31**. See Figure 1.37. Press **Tab**, and the balance sheet as of 10/31/95 appears along with a column of zeros for the 10/31/94 balance sheet.

Date has changed in the "As of" box

Figure 1.37

Preliminary Balance Sheet as of 10/31/95

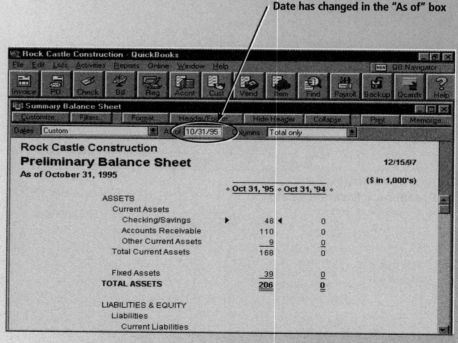

2 Click the **Customize** button on the Report button bar.

3 Unclick the **Previous Year** check box you saw in Figure 1.33 to hide the previous year's figures on the balance sheet.

Jim now wants to print this balance sheet as of October 31, 1995 so he can fax it to Francis.

PRINTING THE BALANCE SHEET
. . . .

You print a balance sheet just as you print any other report in QuickBooks.

To print the Summary Balance Sheet report:

1 Click **Print** on the Summary Balance Sheet button bar.

2 Click **Print** in the Print Reports dialog box to print the report. See Figure 1.38.

Rock Castle Construction
Preliminary Balance Sheet
As of October 31, 1995

	Oct 31, '95
ASSETS	
Current Assets	48
Accounts Receivable	110
Other Current Assets	9
Total Current Assets	168
Fixed Assets	39
TOTAL ASSETS	206
LIABILITIES & EQUITY	
Liabilities	
Current Liabilities	
Accounts Payable	54
Credit Cards	0
Other Current Liabilities	15
Total Current Liabilities	69
Long Term Liabilities	40
Total Liabilities	109
Equity	97
TOTAL LIABILITIES & EQUITY	206

Figure 1.38
Printed Preliminary Balance Sheet

3 Close all windows and, if you are not proceeding to Session 3, exit QuickBooks.

Jim feels much more confident about creating the year-end balance sheet in a couple of weeks. And you are quickly becoming more comfortable with QuickBooks.

practice

session

2

Session 2 Questions

1 List the preset ways in which QuickBooks can present a balance sheet.

2 What time period alternatives does QuickBooks provide for a balance sheet?

3 List the steps you would take to create a balance sheet for a date other than the current system date.

4 Describe the steps to generate a balance sheet in QuickBooks.

5 Describe the steps to reformat the columns of a comparative balance sheet.

6 Describe the different types of transactions you might find in a Transactions by Account report on accounts receivable.

7 Describe how QuickZoom gives you more information about a balance sheet.

8 How might a manager use QuickZoom to analyze a business' financial position as reported in a balance sheet?

9 List five ways you can customize a QuickBooks report.

10 Suppose you wanted to include a column in a balance sheet that described what percentage each asset, liability, and owners' equity account was of the total assets amount. How would you do this in QuickBooks?

Session 2 Assignments

1 *Creating a Customized Comparative Balance Sheet for Rock Castle*

Jim Reed asks you to help him prepare a balance sheet.

   a. He asks you to prepare and print a customized summary balance sheet as of November 30, 1995. He wants the amounts represented in thousands. Don't click the without cents checkbox and make sure to select the summary balance sheet and not standard.

   b. Jim also asks you to prepare and print a summary balance sheet for Rock Castle Construction Company as of July 31, 1995. He wants amounts to be displayed without cents and the page layout left-aligned.

2 *Investigating the Rock Castle Balance Sheet Using QuickZoom*

Jim Reed asks you to help him investigate the Accounts Receivable balance as of December 15, 1995.

a. Create a summary balance sheet as of December 15, 1995.

b. Investigate the Accounts Receivable balance.

c. Examine and print a copy of Invoice 133.

d. What was the invoice date and invoice number related to the September 9, 1995 customer payment?

3 *Using the South-Western Home Page for More Assignments or Cases*

If you have Internet access, go to the home page for this textbook at **owen.swcollege.com**.

Select the **Chapter 1 Session 2** section, and complete the problem(s) your instructor assigns.

Go to **owen.swcollege.com**

http://

4 *Customizing a Balance Sheet*

Modify the balance sheet you created in Assignment 1a to include columns reporting each asset, liability, and owners' equity account as a percentage of total assets. Change the report title and format the page as shown in Figure 1.39.

12/15/95

($ in 1,000's)

Rock Castle Construction
Statement of Financial Position
As of November 30, 1995

	Nov 30, '95	% of Column
ASSETS		
Current Assets		
Checking/Savings		
Checking	39	19%
Total Checking/Savings	39	19%
Accounts Receivable		
Accounts Receivable	116	57%
Total Accounts Receivable	116	57%

Figure 1.39

Customized Balance Sheet for November 30, 1995

Session 2 Case Problem: JENNINGS & ASSOCIATES

Kelly Jennings has just started working full-time in her new business— an advertising agency named Jennings & Associates located in San Martin, California. Like many eager entrepreneurs, she started her business while working full-time for another firm. At first, her billings were quite small. But as her client base and her billings grew, she decided to leave her job and set out on her own. Two of her colleagues and friends—Cheryl Boudreau and Diane Murphy—see Kelly's eagerness and dedication, and decide the time is right for them too. They ask Kelly if they can join her sole proprietorship as employees, and so together they leave the traditional corporate agency environment.

Kelly knows that one of the first tasks she must accomplish is to set up an accounting system for Jennings & Associates. Also, she has just received a request from her banker to submit a balance sheet as documentation for a business loan. As a close, personal friend, you recommend she use QuickBooks, and you volunteer to help her get started.

Kelly tells you that in 1996 she borrowed $5,000 to start the business. Now she is applying for a loan to help expand the business. She also reminds you that although she did conduct some business in 1996, her first full-time month was January 1997.

Prepare and print the following reports using kj01cp.qbw, located on your Student Disk:

1 A standard balance sheet as of December 31, 1996.
2 A standard balance sheet as of January 31, 1997.
3 An itemized balance sheet for the month of January 1997.
4 A summary balance sheet as of January 31, 1997 formatted in thousands and without cents.
5 A report of those transactions recorded in January 1997 that affected accounts payable. (*Hint:* Create a summary balance sheet and double-click **Accounts Payable**.)

Preparing an Income Statement Using QuickBooks

3

Learning Objectives

In this session you will:

- Create income statements for different time periods
- Create an income statement with year-to-date comparative information
- Investigate the detail underlying income statement items
- Use the Income Statement Report button bars
- Print an income statement

CASE: ROCK CASTLE CONSTRUCTION COMPANY

Now that Jim has created a preliminary balance sheet, he wants to practice for the year-end closing by creating a preliminary income statement for the period January 1, 1995 through December 15, 1995. You recall from your accounting course that the income statement reports revenues and expenses for a specific period of time.

Again, as part of your training with QuickBooks, Jim asks you to watch how he prepares the preliminary income statement. He expects to use many of the same functions and features to prepare an income statement that he used to prepare the balance sheet.

CREATING AN INCOME STATEMENT

As with the Balance Sheet and other reports available in QuickBooks, the income statement can be presented in preset ways and can be customized. Jim decides to examine one of the preset income statement formats first—the format called Standard.

Before he does, he calls your attention to the fact that QuickBooks does not use the traditional name for this report. Instead of calling it the income statement, QuickBooks refers to this report as the "Profit and Loss" report. Jim prefers the name "income statement" because it is really the most accurate name for this report. And he says that although he cannot change the report title on the menu, he'll show you later how you can change the title on the report itself.

To create a standard income statement:

1 Open rock.qbw.

2 Click **Reports**, click **Profit and Loss**, and then click **Standard**. Change the From date to 12/01/95 and the To date to 12/15/95. Click once. See Figure 1.40.

CHANGE DATE

Called "Income Statement" in traditional accounting

Figure 1.40

A Rock Castle Income Statement for the Period December 1, 1995 to December 15, 1995

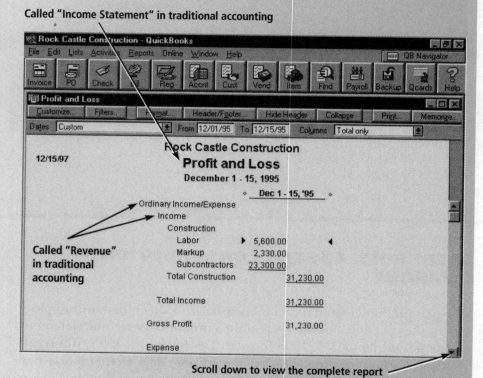

Called "Revenue" in traditional accounting

Scroll down to view the complete report

3 Scroll down the Rock Castle Construction Company income statement. This report summarizes revenues and expenses for this month-to-date. Notice that QuickBooks does not use the standard accounting term "revenue," but instead uses the term "income." Note that subtotals are included for revenues and expenses. Note also the period specified for this particular report is December 1–15, 1995, the period for this month-to-date.

Jim tells you that this report is too limited. He wants a year-to-date statement for his preliminary income statement.

CREATING AN INCOME STATEMENT FOR A SPECIFIED PERIOD

As you have just seen, the default setting for QuickBooks creates an income statement for the current month with the period ending as of the system date. In the example files for Rock Castle, the current month and date were December 1995. But you will rarely need an income statement for the month ending with the system date. Thus you will often need to change the date specified in the income statement's From and To fields to the dates you want. Jim decides to revise the report to make it a year-to-date income statement for the period January 1, 1995 through December 15, 1995. He also wants to show you how to change the report title from "Profit and Loss" to the more accurate "Income Statement." For this title change you will modify the header, a function you already learned how to perform with the balance sheet.

To revise the period of time and the report title:

1 Move the cursor to the From field, which appears directly below the Header/Footer button on the Report button bar. Delete 12 and type **01**. Move the cursor anywhere in the report, and click once to refresh the screen. The revised report appears. See Figure 1.41.

Changed date to 01/01/95

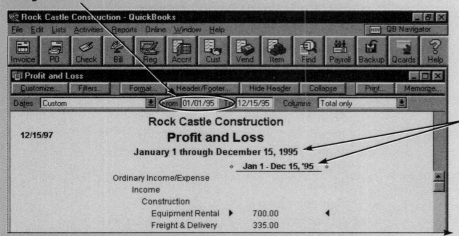

Figure 1.41

The Revised Income Statement for the Period January 1 to December 15, 1995

Titles change with From/To date change

2 To change the report title, click **Header/Footer** on the Report button bar. The Format Header/Footer window appears. See Figure 1.42.

3 Move the cursor to the Report Title edit box and delete Profit and Loss. Type **Income Statement**.

4 Click **OK** to view the revised report. See Figure 1.43.

5 When you have finished viewing the revised report, close this window.

Figure 1.42
*The Format Header/Footer
Window*

Figure 1.43
*Revised Rock Castle
Income Statement
with Corrected Title*

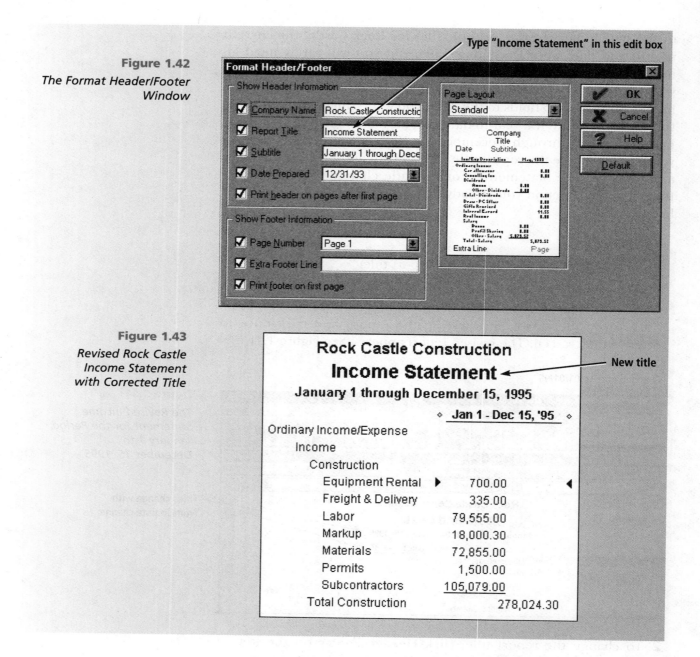

Type "Income Statement" in this edit box

New title

Once again Jim comments on how remarkably fast this process is compared to creating income statements manually. As with the balance sheet, he decides to create a year-to-date comparison—this time with the income statement.

CREATING A COMPARATIVE INCOME STATEMENT

QuickBooks has a built-in feature to prepare comparative income statements easily and quickly if the comparative data has already been entered into a QuickBooks file. Jim entered last year's income statement data when he first created rock.qbw, so he is ready to create the comparative income statement. You guess that the process will be very similar to how you already prepared the comparative balance sheet.

To create a comparative income statement for the year-to-date period ended December 15, 1995:

1 Click **Reports**, click **Profit and Loss**, and then click **Prev Year Comparison**. Note that the standard accounting term is "comparative" income statement not "comparison," the term QuickBooks uses. Figure 1.44 appears. In the From and To boxes change the year to 1995, and click once in the report.

CHANGE DATE

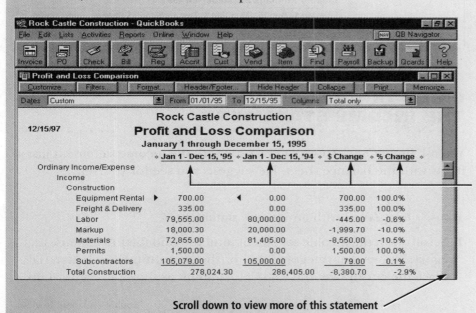

Figure 1.44

QuickBooks's Comparison Income Statement Report for Rock Castle for the Periods January 1 to December 15 for 1995 and 1994

4-column comparison

Scroll down to view more of this statement

trouble? If your screen does not look the same as Figure 1.44, the column widths are probably not the same. As you learned in Session 2, you can change the column widths by dragging the small diamond-shaped symbols that divide the columns. If a dialog box appears asking if you want to make all columns the same width, you may answer yes or no.

2 Scroll down and across this comparative income statement. Note that it includes four columns. The first two columns compare amounts for 1995 with 1994, respectively, for the current period. The other two columns show the change in dollar amount and percent.

trouble? If the first two column headings omit the years 1995 and 1994, it's probably because you have changed the column widths in such a way that the complete column heading is not displayed. The first column is for 1995 and the second is for 1994.

Now Jim wants to change the title of the report to conform to standard accounting terminology.

To change the title of the report:

1 Click **Header/Footer** on the Report button bar. The Format Header/Footer window appears.

2 Delete "Profit and Loss Comparison" in the Report Title edit box, and type **Comparative Income Statement**.

3 Click **OK** to view the revised report. See Figure 1.45.

Figure 1.45

Comparative Year-to-Date Income Statement with Corrected Title

Changed title

Rock Castle Construction
Comparative Income Statement
January 1 through December 15, 1995

	Jan 1 - Dec 15, '95	Jan 1 - Dec 15, '94	$ Change	% Change

Ordinary Income/Expense
  Income

USING QUICKZOOM WITH THE INCOME STATEMENT

You ask Jim if QuickZoom can be used with the income statement just as it was with the balance sheet. He suggests you see for yourself.

To use QuickZoom with an income statement:

1 Scroll down the income statement until you find the Job Expenses category. Under that category look for the account titled Job Materials. Place the cursor over the 75,841.15 amount as shown in Figure 1.46.

Figure 1.46

Using QuickZoom to View the Job Materials Expense for 1995

Double-click here to view detailed transactions for job materials

Expense category

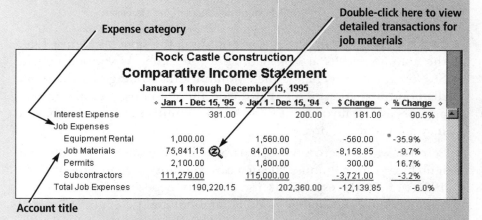

Account title

	Jan 1 - Dec 15, '95	Jan 1 - Dec 15, '94	$ Change	% Change
Interest Expense	381.00	200.00	181.00	90.5%
Job Expenses				
Equipment Rental	1,000.00	1,560.00	-560.00	-35.9%
Job Materials	75,841.15	84,000.00	-8,158.85	-9.7%
Permits	2,100.00	1,800.00	300.00	16.7%
Subcontractors	111,279.00	115,000.00	-3,721.00	-3.2%
Total Job Expenses	190,220.15	202,360.00	-12,139.85	-6.0%

2 Double-click the **75,841.15** amount. A report appears that provides the details of transactions by account. See Figure 1.47. This particular report displays the transactions that increased the job materials expense from 1/01/95 to 12/15/95.

Double-click here to view the detail of this transaction

Figure 1.47

Transactions Detail for the Job Materials Account in 1995

3 Double-click **Cabinets** in the first transaction listed, or any other word in this row. Figure 1.48 appears. It is a bill dated 6/9/95 from Sarvis Kitchen and Bath for a total of $3,630.

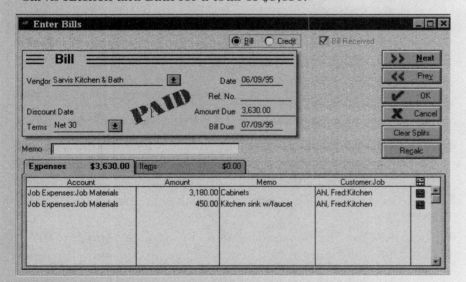

Figure 1.48

Sarvis Kitchen and Bath Bill

4 After you view this bill, close all windows.

You have now seen that the QuickZoom feature of QuickBooks is available with the income statement as well as with the balance sheet and that it provides background detail relating to revenues and expenses.

CUSTOMIZING THE INCOME STATEMENT REPORT

The Income Statement report, like all other reports created in QuickBooks, can be customized using the Report button bar. Jim knows from experience that when he works with income statements in the future he will definitely need to add columns, change report dates, use different number formats, modify headings, and so on. So he decides to explore the ways he can customize an income statement. He decides first to add percentage of net income columns and change the report dates.

To add percentage of net income columns and to change the dates on an Income Statement report:

1 Click **Reports**, click **Profit and Loss**, and then click **Standard**.

2 Click the **Customize** button on the Report button bar.

3 Click the **Down Arrow** of the **Columns** drop-down edit box, and select **Month** to report monthly columns. See Figure 1.49.

Change this to "Month" to modify column configuration

Change to these dates to customize the report

Figure 1.49

The Customize Report Window

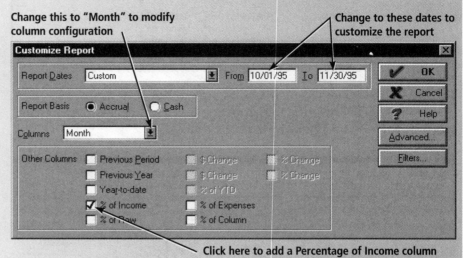

Click here to add a Percentage of Income column

4 Click the **% of Income** check box under **Other Columns** to report monthly amounts as a percent of total income—actually a percent of total revenue. See Figure 1.49.

CHANGE DATE

5 Click the **From** edit box and change the date from 12/01/97 to **10/01/95**.

CHANGE DATE

6 Click the **To** edit box and change the date from 12/15/97 to **11/30/95**. See Figure 1.49. These two changes customize the report so it reports on the months of October and November only.

7 Click **OK** to accept these changes. A revised report appears. See Figure 1.50. Adjust the column widths if necessary to view more of the report.

Figure 1.50

The Rock Castle Comparative Income Statement with New Columns and New Dates

New dates

Percentage columns

Rock Castle Construction
Profit and Loss
October through November 1995

	Oct '95	% of Income	Nov '95	% of Income
Ordinary Income/Expense				
Income				
Construction				
Equipment Rental ▶	0.00 ◀	0.0%	1,000.00	2.9%
Freight & Delivery	75.00	0.2%	125.00	0.4%
Labor	8,400.00	22.8%	9,800.00	28%
Markup	2,528.50	6.9%	2,282.00	6.5%
Materials	16,245.00	44.2%	11,855.00	33.9%
Permits	300.00	0.8%	300.00	0.9%
Subcontractors	9,235.00	25.1%	9,600.00	27.5%
Total Construction	36,783.50	100.0%	34,962.00	100.0%

Jim decides that he wants to report the numbers without cents.

To report the amounts without cents:

1 Click **Format** on the Report button bar. The Format Report window appears.

2 Click the **Without Cents** check box under the Show All Numbers section of the Format Report window. A check mark appears in the box.

3 Click **OK** to accept these changes. The revised report appears. See Figure 1.51.

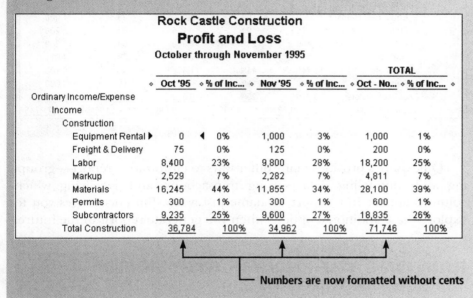

Figure 1.51
The Rock Castle Comparative Income Statement with Numbers Reported without Cents

As Jim looks over the latest version of the income statement, he sees that again he must correct the report title. Also, he decides the title would look better if it appeared on the right side of the report.

To modify the title and its layout:

1 Click the **Header/Footer** button on the Report button bar.

2 Click inside the **Report Title** edit box, and change the name of the report from "Profit and Loss" to "Income Statement" as you have done before.

3 Change the title layout by clicking the **Down Arrow** in the Page Layout section and changing the selection from Standard to **Right**.

4 Before you accept these changes, look at the Subtitle edit box. Notice that QuickBooks has changed the subtitle of this report. QuickBooks does this automatically for you whenever you change the dates in the To and From edit boxes.

5 Click **OK** to accept the changes. The customized income statement appears. See Figure 1.52.

Figure 1.52

The Customized Income Statement Report with New Title and Right Page Layout

Right justified report title

	Oct '95	% of Income	Nov '95	% of Income	TOTAL Oct - Nov '...
Rock Castle Construction					
Income Statement					
October through November 1995					
Ordinary Income/Expense					
Income					
Construction					
Equipment Rental ▶	0	◀ 0%	1,000	3%	1,000
Freight & Delivery	75	0%	125	0%	200
Labor	8,400	23%	9,800	28%	18,200
Markup	2,529	7%	2,282	7%	4,811
Materials	16,245	44%	11,855	34%	28,100
Permits	300	1%	300	1%	600
Subcontractors	9,235	25%	9,600	27%	18,835
Total Construction	36,784	100%	34,962	100%	71,746

QuickBooks provides many other ways to customize a report—grouping and subtotaling data, sorting transactions, and specifying which columns appear in a report, to name just a few. Jim encourages you to explore these additional options when you generate reports in the future.

PRINTING THE INCOME STATEMENT

Jim would like to print this customized report so he can show some of the managers at Rock Castle an example of the type of reports he can generate for them. He'd like this example to fit on one piece of 8$\frac{1}{2}$" x 11" paper—both to save paper and to make analysis of the report easier. He decides to use QuickBooks's preview option to preview the report and see if it will fit onto one piece of paper.

To preview the customized income statement:

1 Click **Print** on the Report button bar.

2 Click **Preview** in the Print Reports window. A miniature reproduction of the report appears. See Figure 1.53. (Do not resize the columns.) Notice the heading "Page 1 of 2" at the top of the window. This indicates how many pages the report contains and which page you are previewing.

trouble? Your screen may indicate Page 1 of 1 depending on your computer and printer settings. If so, skip to Step 4, but continue reading so that you are familiar with the options that can help fit a long report on one page.

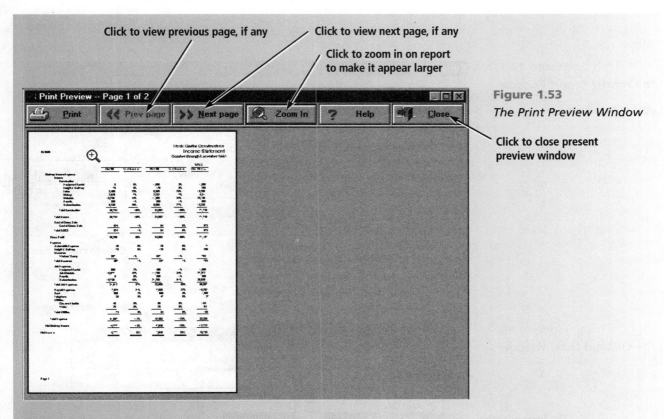

Click to view previous page, if any

Click to view next page, if any

Click to zoom in on report to make it appear larger

Figure 1.53
The Print Preview Window

Click to close present preview window

3 Notice the Next page and Prev page buttons below the window heading. The Prev page button is grayed out, which indicates that there is no previous page. But the Next page button is not grayed out. Click **Next page** to preview Page 2 of the report.

4 After previewing the statement, click the **Close** button on the button bar, and then click **Cancel** in the Print Reports window. The report reappears.

Jim has seen that the report is not much more than one page and so it might fit onto one page if he reduces the size of the type font.

To reduce the font size of the type in a report:

1 Click **Format** on the Report button bar. The Format Report window appears. See Figure 1.54.

2 Click the **Change Font** button located in the bottom center of the window. The Column Labels window appears. See Figure 1.55.

3 Click the **Size** edit box. Delete 9 and type (or click on) **8** to reduce the font size by one. Then click the **Font** edit box and choose **Arial Narrow,** if available, or choose another font that is small enough to accomplish your goal.

Figure 1.54

The Format Report Window

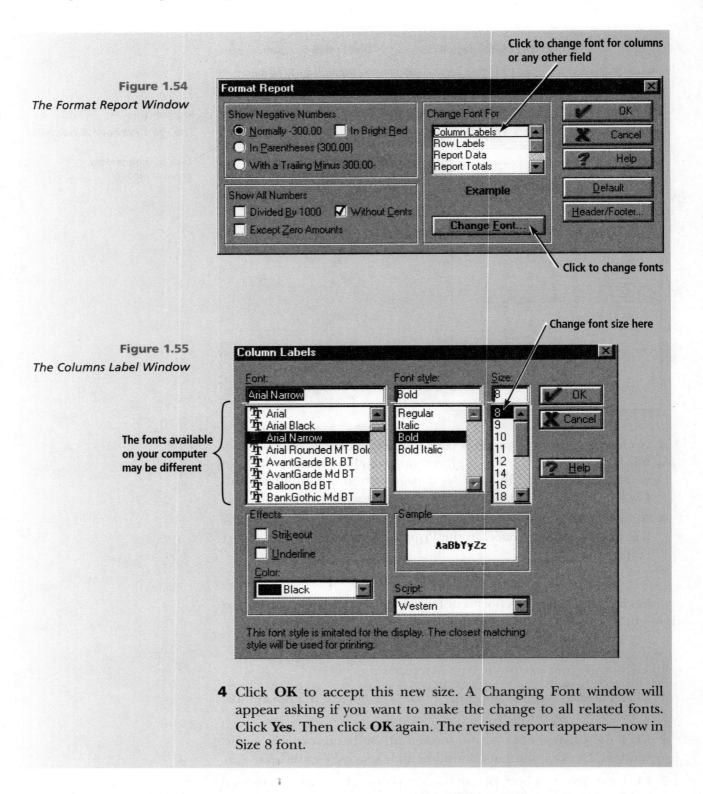

Click to change font for columns
or any other field

Click to change fonts

Change font size here

Figure 1.55

The Columns Label Window

The fonts available
on your computer
may be different

4 Click **OK** to accept this new size. A Changing Font window will
appear asking if you want to make the change to all related fonts.
Click **Yes**. Then click **OK** again. The revised report appears—now in
Size 8 font.

Jim hopes that this change will make the example report now fit on
one page. To see if it worked, he again previews the report. If it fits on
one page, he'll print it.

To preview the customized income statement again:

1 Click **Print** on the Report button bar.

2 Click **Preview**. The Print Preview window appears. Notice that the heading for this window still includes the words "Page 1 of 2." The change of font size has reduced the report size but not adequately to fit the report on one page.

3 Click **Close**, and then click **Cancel** in the Print Reports window.

Suddenly Jim realizes there might be another way to fit the report on one page. He decides to change the orientation of the page from portrait—a vertical orientation—which is the default setting, to landscape—a horizontal orientation.

To change a document from portrait to landscape orientation:

1 Click **Print** on the Report button bar to view the Print Reports window. See Figure 1.56.

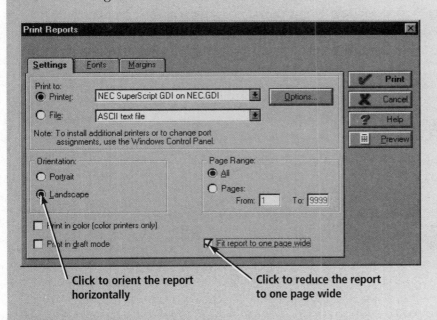

Figure 1.56
The Print Report window

2 Click **Landscape**.

3 Click **Fit report to one page wide**.

4 Click **Preview** once again. The report now fits on one page.

5 Click **Print** from the Print Preview window. Your completed report should look like Figure 1.57 as shown on the next page.

trouble? If by chance your printer still prints this document on two pages consult with your lab personnel. Different printers may result in different output.

6 Close all windows and exit QuickBooks as you have done before.

Figure 1.57 *Jim's Customized Example Income Statement on One Page*

12/15/95

Rock Castle Construction
Income Statement
October through November 1995

	Oct '95	% of Income	Nov '95	% of Income	Oct-Nov '95 TOTAL	% of Income
Ordinary Income/Expense						
Income						
Construction						
Equipment Rental	0	0%	1,000	3%	1,000	1%
Freight & Delivery	75	0%	125	0%	200	0%
Labor	8,400	23%	9,800	28%	18,200	25%
Markup	2,528	7%	2,282	7%	4,811	7%
Materials	16,245	44%	11,855	34%	28,100	39%
Permits	300	1%	300	1%	600	1%
Subcontractors	9,235	25%	9,600	27%	18,835	26%
Total Construction	36,784	100%	34,962	100%	71,746	100%
Total Income	36,784	100%	34,962	100%	71,746	100%
Cost of Goods Sold						
Cost of Goods Sold	524	1%	54	0%	578	1%
Total COGS	524	1%	54	0%	578	1%
Gross Profit	36,259	99%	34,908	100%	71,167	99%
Expense						
Automobile Expense	45	0%	26	0%	71	0%
Freight & Delivery	75	0%	125	0%	200	0%
Insurance						
Workers' Comp	367	1%	337	1%	704	1%
Total Insurance	367	1%	337	1%	704	1%
Job Expenses						
Equipment Rental	600	2%	400	1%	1,000	1%
Job Materials	15,577	42%	11,795	34%	27,372	38%
Permits	0	0%	300	1%	300	0%
Subcontractors	15,735	43%	21,200	61%	36,935	51%
Total Job Expenses	31,912	87%	33,695	96%	65,607	91%
Payroll Expenses	7,624	21%	7,639	22%	15,262	21%
Rent	900	2%	900	3%	1,800	3%
Telephone	39	0%	47	0%	87	0%
Utilities						
Gas and Electric	49	0%	55	0%	104	0%
Water	25	0%	29	0%	54	0%
Total Utilities	74	0%	84	0%	158	0%
Total Expense	41,037	112%	42,853	123%	83,889	117%
Net Ordinary Income	-4,777	-13%	-7,945	-23%	-12,722	-18%
Net Income	**-4,777**	**-13%**	**-7,945**	**-23%**	**-12,722**	**-18%**

Now that you have completed Sessions 2 and 3 of Chapter 1, you see how easily QuickBooks creates the two financial reports most commonly used to communicate accounting information to external users—the balance sheet and the income statement. In Session 4 of Chapter 1, you will complete your quick overview of QuickBooks by creating supporting reports for accounts receivable, inventory, and accounts payable.

practice

3

Session 3 Questions

1 List at least three of the preset formats QuickBooks provides for an income statement.

2 Identify the different periods of time that QuickBooks provides for an income statement.

3 Describe the steps necessary to create an income statement for a period other than one ending with the current system date of the computer.

4 Describe the steps necessary to generate an income statement in QuickBooks.

5 Describe the steps necessary to reformat the columns of a comparative income statement.

6 Describe the steps necessary to customize an income statement to include comparative information.

7 How does QuickZoom help you further investigate an income statement?

8 How could a manager use QuickZoom to access underlying information as reported in an income statement?

9 List five report customization features that QuickBooks provides with an income statement.

10 How would you customize an income statement to include a column describing the percentage relationship between expenses and total revenues?

Session 3 Assignments

1 *Preparing an Income Statement for Rock Castle*

Jim Reed has asked you to help him prepare Rock Castle's income statement.

a. First he asks you to prepare and print a customized income statement that includes operating information for August and September 1995. He wants the income statement to include amounts (without cents) and columns reflecting the dollar change and percentage change between periods. *Hint:* Set the dates to reflect September only, and be sure the Previous Period box, $ Change, and % Change boxes are also checked in the Customize Report window. He asks you to change the title to "Income Statement Comparison." Finally, he wants you to format the page layout to the left.

b. Next Jim asks you to prepare and print a summary income statement for Rock Castle Construction Company for the month ended July 31, 1995 in a different format than you used in *a* above.

2 *Investigating the Rock Castle Income Statement Using QuickZoom*

Jim Reed asks you to help him investigate the $111,279 Job Expense:Subcontractors balance shown on a standard income statement created for the fiscal year ended December 15, 1995.

a. Create a standard income statement for the fiscal year ended December 15, 1995.
b. Investigate the $111,279 Job Expense:Subcontractors.
   trouble? Remember to change the From/To dates on the income statement to reflect the fiscal year-to-date amounts.
c. Examine the bill received on June 1, 1995.
d. Which vendor performed the work?
e. Has the bill been paid?

3 *Using the South-Western Home Page for More Assignments or Cases*

If you have Internet access, go to the home page for this textbook at owen.swcollege.com.
   Select the **Chapter 1 Session 3** section, and complete the problem(s) that your instructor assigns.

Go to
owen.swcollege.com

http://

4 *Customizing an Income Statement*

Customize the income statement created in Chapter Assignment 1 as follows:

a. Change the To/From dates to include amounts from October 1 through December 15, 1995.
b. Change the columns to no longer reflect comparative information.
c. Change the columns to include year-to-date amounts and year-to-date percentages. *Hint:* Customize the report by checking the Year-to-Date and % of YTD boxes.
d. Print this customized income statement.

Session 3 Case Problem: JENNINGS & ASSOCIATES

As you learned in Session 2, Kelly Jennings prepared a balance sheet to submit to her banker with her application for a business loan. When she delivered the balance sheet to the banker, he told her that he also needed information about her operations. In other words, her banker needed an income statement.

Kelly asks you to help her prepare three versions of the income statement, one of which she will include with her application. She gives you a QuickBooks file named kj01cp.qbw.

1 Open kj01cp.qbw from your Student Disk.

2 Prepare a standard income statement for the month of January 1997.

3 Prepare a standard income statement for the month of January 1997 without cents, formatted with a left layout, and with the title "Income Statement."

4 Modify the income statement you prepared for *3* above by adding a % of Income column.

Creating Supporting Reports to Help Make Business Decisions

4

Learning Objectives

In this session you will:

- Create, print, and analyze an Accounts Receivable Aging report
- Create and print a Customer Account Balance Summary
- Create, print, and analyze an Inventory Valuation Summary
- Create, print, and analyze an Accounts Payable Aging report
- Create and print a Vendor Balance Summary

CASE: ROCK CASTLE CONSTRUCTION COMPANY

You arrive at work, and two phones are ringing. As Jim hangs up from one call and is about to answer another, he quickly explains what's happening—the managers at Rock Castle are preparing for the fiscal year-end and are requesting up-to-the-minute information. You quickly answer a phone and write down the manager's request for some information on inventory. As you hang up from the call, Jim asks you to come into his office. You compare notes—he has requests for information on accounts receivable and accounts payable. You show him your note requesting information on Rock Castle's inventory.

Jim has shown you that QuickBooks can easily generate transaction reports, but you can see that the manager's requests require more detailed information. You remember from your accounting course that accountants frequently use what are called **supporting schedules**—reports that provide the underlying details of an account. You ask Jim if QuickBooks can help. He smiles and says, "You bet. QuickBooks calls these schedules 'reports,' but they are the same thing. Let's get to work."

CREATING AND PRINTING AN ACCOUNTS RECEIVABLE AGING REPORT

You know from your accounting course that accounts receivable represent amounts due from customers for goods or services they have received but for which they have not yet paid. QuickBooks provides several preset accounts receivable reports that anticipate the information managers most often need.

The first request for information is from Susan Guttmann, the manager in charge of accounts receivable. She wants information on a particular customer's past due account balance, and she wants to know the total amount due from customers as of today.

Jim tells you that the best way to get information on past due accounts is to create a schedule that QuickBooks calls an "Accounts Receivable Aging report"—but what you learned in your accounting course is usually called an "accounts receivable aging schedule." You remember that an aging schedule is a listing of how long each receivable has been uncollected.

To create an Accounts Receivable Aging report:

1 Open rock.qbw located on your Student Disk.

2 Click **Reports** and then click **A/R Reports**. A submenu appears.

3 Click **Aging Summary** on this submenu. An Accounts Receivable Aging report appears. Change the date to 12/15/95 and click once. See Figure 1.58.

CHANGE DATE

Figure 1.58

Rock Castle's A/R Aging Summary as of 12/15/95

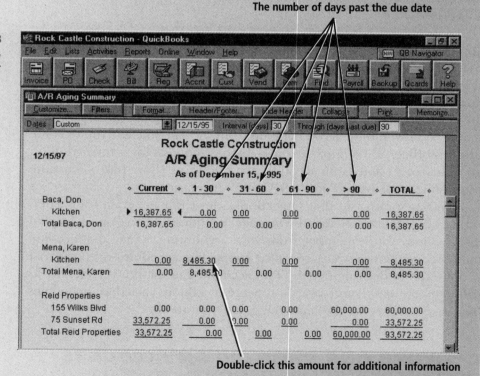

4 If necessary, resize the columns so you can view the entire report on your screen.

You can see that this report gives Susan an up-to-date listing of customers and their balances. It tells her how long each receivable has been uncollected so she can take appropriate action.

You ask Jim the name of the customer about whom Susan requested information. He says the customer's name is Karen Mena and that Susan wants to know the status of her account and her payment history. He says that, as you have done with other reports, you can use QuickZoom to gather this information.

To investigate a particular receivable on an Accounts Receivable Aging report:

1 Double-click the **8,485.30** balance owed by Karen Mena.

2 An A/R Aging QuickZoom report appears. See Figure 1.59. This report indicates that Invoice 134, dated 10/20/95, was due 11/19/95 and is presently 26 days late.

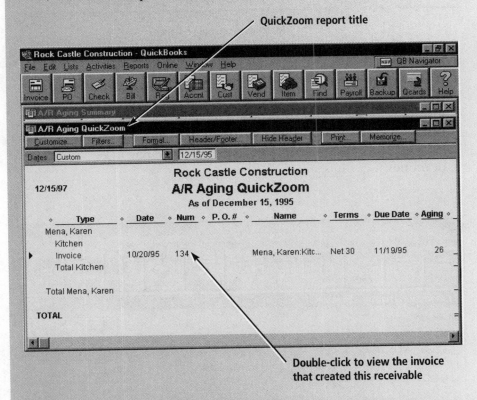

Figure 1.59

A/R Aging QuickZoom Report

3 Double-click **134** to investigate further. Invoice 134 appears. See Figure 1.60. Invoice 134 describes the framing labor, installation labor, and reimbursable expenses that Rock Castle billed Karen Mena. Adjust the size of your window if necessary to view the entire window.

4 Click the **Down Arrow** in the invoice's scroll box to view more of the invoice. Notice that the balance due—8,485.30—matches the receivable balance you are investigating. But notice also that Invoice 134 totals 17,669.92. How can that be?

Figure 1.60

Invoice 134

Click to display
payment history
for this invoice

Click to scroll up
or down the
invoice data

Invoice total
differs from
balance due

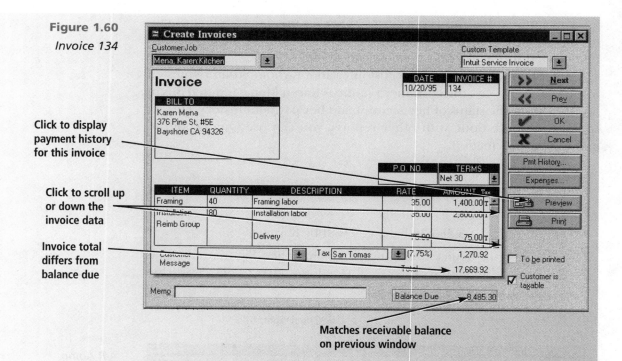

Matches receivable balance
on previous window

5 Click the **Pmt History** button on the right side of the window to help
you investigate this difference. The transaction history of this
invoice appears. See Figure 1.61. Notice that a payment of 9,184.62
was applied to this invoice on 12/01/95. This seems an unusual
amount for a customer to pay; usually people pay in even amounts
of money. Let's investigate further.

Figure 1.61

*Invoice 134
Transaction History*

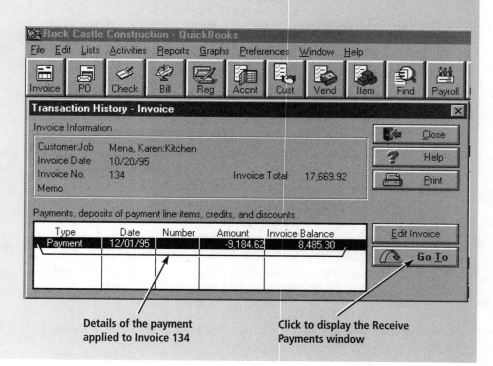

Details of the payment
applied to Invoice 134

Click to display the Receive
Payments window

6 Be sure that the 9,184.62 payment is highlighted. Then click **Go To** to examine the payment in more detail. The Receive Payments window appears. See Figure 1.62. Notice that a $10,000 check was received from Karen Mena on 12/01/95. Of this payment, $815.38 was applied to pay off Invoice 133. The balance of the $10,000.00—9,184.62—was applied to Invoice 134. This explains why the balance due and the invoice amount were different.

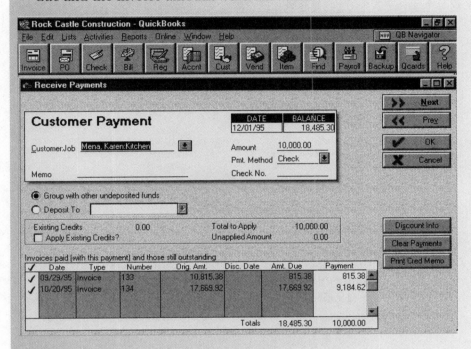

Figure 1.62
Receive Payments Window for Karen Mena

7 Close all open windows.

Jim has copied down the information Susan requested—Karen Mena is 26 days past due on Invoice 134, she owes $8,485.30 on that invoice, and Invoice 133 was paid off on 12/01/95. He is now ready to fulfill Susan's other request.

CREATING AND PRINTING A CUSTOMER BALANCE SUMMARY

Jim says that Susan's request for the total amount due from customers as of today is easy to fulfill, because QuickBooks has a built-in feature that prepares a customer balance summary. He can provide Susan this information with only a few clicks of the mouse.

To create a Customer Balance Summary:

1 Click **Reports**, then click **A/R Reports**. Click **Customer Balance Summary** from the submenu. The Customer Balance Summary appears. See Figure 1.63.

Figure 1.63

Customer Balance Summary for December 15, 1995

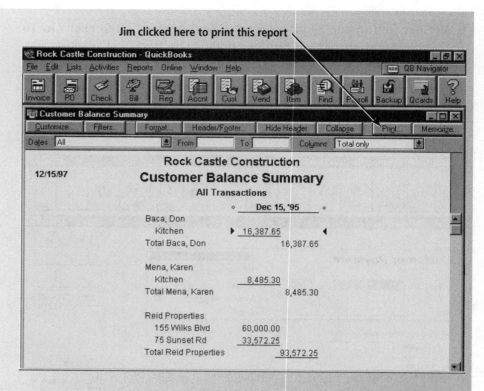

2 Notice that this is exactly the information Susan has requested—a list of the total amounts each customer owes Rock Castle as of December 15, 1995. When you have finished viewing this report, close this window.

Jim prints this report for Susan and asks you to drop it by her desk later. He's ready to handle the second request.

CREATING AND PRINTING AN INVENTORY VALUATION SUMMARY REPORT

Jim asks you about the request you took on the phone. You show him your notes; you spoke to Kim Hui, who handles inventory for Rock Castle. Occasionally, when he finds good prices, Kim purchases inventory materials that Rock Castle routinely uses—such as doorknobs, locks, and nails—and he holds them for future jobs. For the fiscal-year-end planning and reporting, Kim wants to know what inventory Rock Castle has on hand, its acquisition cost, and recent sales.

Jim tells you that, again, QuickBooks has a report that anticipates many of the information needs of inventory managers. He says you can easily get the information Kim needs by creating what QuickBooks calls an Inventory Valuation Summary.

To create an Inventory Valuation Summary :

1 Click **Reports**, click **Inventory Reports**, and then click **Valuation Summary** from the submenu. The Inventory Valuation Summary appears. Change the date to 12/15/95 and click once. See Figure 1.64. Resize the columns as necessary to view this report.

CHANGE DATE

Figure 1.64
An Inventory Valuation Summary for Rock Castle

Note the date of this report

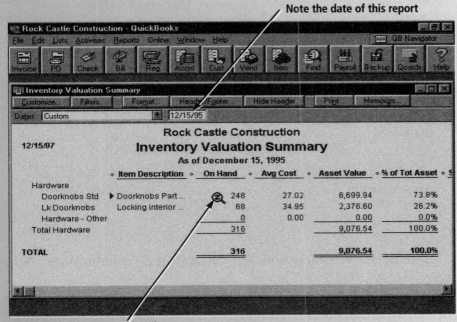

Click to view inventory detail

2 Scroll around this report to familiarize yourself with its contents. It describes the inventory on hand as of 12/15/95.

As you examine this report, you notice that the QuickZoom cursor appears every so often as it passes over certain items. You ask Jim to show you examples of the QuickZoom reports that QuickBooks provides for inventory.

To view the underlying documentation of the Inventory Valuation Summary:

1 Double-click on the **248 Doorknobs Std** in the On Hand column. An Inventory Valuation Detail appears. By default, this report shows activity for the current day only (12/15/95 to 12/15/95). But Kim wants to know the *total* inventory on hand and to see activity for the *entire* year. To find this information you need to change the From date to 1/1/95.

2 Delete the date in the From date edit box and type **1/1/95** in the box. Click once on the report itself. A new report appears. See Figure 1.65. Note that this report shows a beginning inventory of 148, an inventory adjustment of 104, and two invoices for sales of 2 units each.

Figure 1.65

Inventory Valuation Detail from January 1 Through December 15, 1995

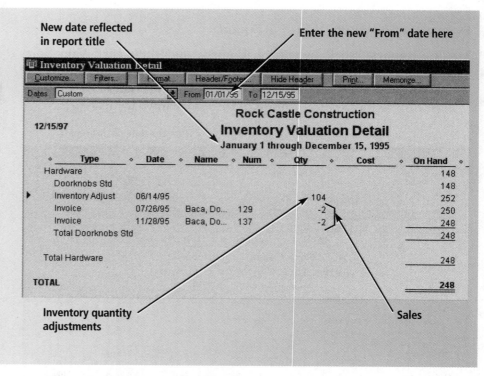

You ask Jim if QuickZoom lets you view the actual invoices. "Sure does," he says. "Let's look at one."

To view an actual invoice:

1 Double-click anywhere in the row containing information on Invoice 137. The invoice appears as shown in Figure 1.66. Adjust your window size or scroll as necessary to view the entire invoice.

Figure 1.66

Invoice 137 Reduced Inventory

Documentation of the two standard doorknobs sold from inventory on 11/28/95

2 After you examine this invoice, close all open windows.

Jim retrieves the Inventory Valuation Summary and prints it for Kim. He asks you to deliver this report to Kim when you deliver Susan's. He's now ready to fulfill the last request.

CREATING, PRINTING, AND ANALYZING AN ACCOUNTS PAYABLE AGING REPORT

The last request to which you and Jim need to respond is from Laura Valdez, accounts payable manager. She wants two reports so she can estimate how much money Rock Castle will owe its vendors at the end of the fiscal year.

You quickly ask if QuickBooks handles accounts payable aging the same way it handles accounts receivable aging. Jim smiles. "You catch on fast," he says. "Let's start with an Accounts Payable Aging report. It provides the detail Laura needs. Then we'll print her a Vendor Balance Summary."

To create an Accounts Payable Aging report:

1 Click **Reports**, click **A/P Reports**, and then click **Aging Summary**. The A/P Aging Summary report appears. Change the date to 12/15/95 and click once. See Figure 1.67.

CHANGE DATE

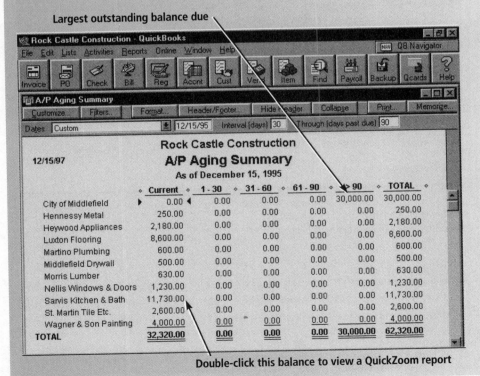

Figure 1.67

Accounts Payable Aging Summary

Largest outstanding balance due

Double-click this balance to view a QuickZoom report

2 Scroll through the A/P Aging Summary. If necessary change the column widths so the entire report displays on your screen.

After Jim prints this report for Laura Valdez, you look it over. You notice a large outstanding balance three months past due to the City of Middlefield, and you suggest using QuickZoom to investigate it further. Jim tells you that Rock Castle is disputing this bill in court and so it's already being handled. You both decide instead to investigate the next largest balance—the Sarvis Kitchen and Bath liability to whom Rock Castle owes $11,730.

To analyze the Sarvis Kitchen and Bath liability:

1 Double-click the Sarvis Kitchen and Bath liability balance of **11,730.00**. An A/P Aging report appears. See Figure 1.68. Notice that two bills are listed; their total is the amount owed to Sarvis as of 12/15/95.

Figure 1.68

A/P Aging QuickZoom Report for Sarvis Kitchen and Bath

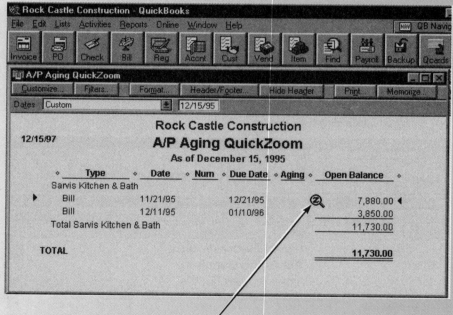

Double-click anywhere on this line to view the underlying bill supporting this entry

2 Double-click anywhere in the entry for the bill dated **11/21/95**. The details of this bill appear. See Figure 1.69. Notice that this bill documents materials expenses incurred in the Don Baca kitchen remodeling job.

3 When you have finished viewing this bill, close all open windows.

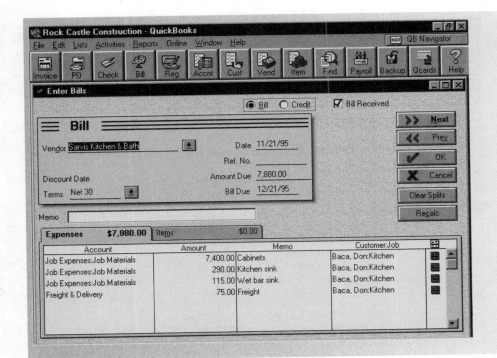

Figure 1.69

*Sarvis Kitchen and Bath
Bill Dated 11/21/95*

CREATING AND PRINTING A VENDOR BALANCE SUMMARY

The final supporting report for Laura Valdez is a Vendor Balance Summary. This report is also a preset report available from the QuickBooks Reports menu. It will summarize for Laura all of the unpaid balances due to vendors and will be valuable information for her year-end reporting.

To create and print a Vendor Balance Summary:

1 Click **Reports**, then **A/P Reports**, and then **Vendor Balance Summary**. The Vendor Balance Summary appears. See Figure 1.70. Notice that the vendors are listed alphabetically.

2 When you finish viewing this report, close this window.

Jim prints the Vendor Balance Summary for Laura, and looks at you. "Yes, I'll deliver this one too," you volunteer good naturedly.

Figure 1.70

Vendor Balance Summary as of December 15, 1995

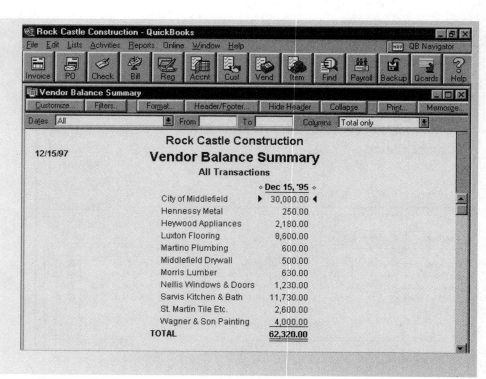

END NOTE

As you gather the reports and set out to deliver them, you are struck by how easily and quickly Jim has been able to respond to the managers' requests. Within a short time, QuickBooks has generated accurate, up-to-the-minute financial information to help Rock Castle's managers. The many preset reports—summaries, details, and supporting documentation—anticipate the information that managers often need to make sound business decisions.

Session 4 Questions

1 Which menu in QuickBooks provides you access to supporting reports?

2 What information does an Accounts Receivable Aging report provide?

3 What types of transactions might appear in a QuickZoom report created from an Accounts Receivable Aging report? Give two examples.

4 How might the payment history of an account receivable help you analyze the Accounts Receivable Aging report?

5 What information does an Inventory Valuation Summary provide?

6 What types of transactions might appear in a QuickZoom report created from an Inventory Summary? Give two examples.

7 What information does an Accounts Payable Aging report provide?

8 What types of transactions might appear in a QuickZoom report created from an Accounts Payable Aging report?

9 What options can you choose from the Print Reports dialog box to help you print a report?

10 How can you create a supporting report for a date other than the system date? Describe a situation for which you would want to do this.

Session 4 Assignments

1 *Creating Supporting Reports for Rock Castle*

Jim Reed wants you to help him provide supporting reports. Use rock.qbw on your Student Disk for this assignment. Create the reports Jim has requested, and write down the answers to the following questions:

a. Create and print a Customer Balance Summary as of 10/31/95. Other than the $60,000 receivable from Reid Properties, what is the amount of the largest customer receivable and what is the customer's name? What invoices support that receivable? What is the nature of each invoice?

b. Create and print an Aging Accounts Receivable report as of 10/31/95. Other than the $60,000 receivable from Reid Properties, list all past due invoices. When is each due? What is the nature of each invoice?

c. Create and print an Aging Accounts Payable report as of 10/31/95. Other than the $30,000 payable to the City of Middlefield, what is the largest vendor liability? What bill makes up this liability? What is the nature of this bill?

d. Create and print an Inventory Valuation Summary as of 10/31/95. What inventory items are on hand? What is their average cost and retail value?

2 *Creating More Supporting Reports for Rock Castle*

Jim Reed wants you to help him provide more supporting reports. Use rock.qbw on your Student Disk for this assignment. Create the reports Jim has requested, and write down the answers to the following questions:

a. Create and print a Customer Balance Summary as of 12/15/95 using All in the dates box and examine the QuickZoom reports for Don Baca. What invoice created this receivable? What was Don Baca invoiced for? What are the terms of this invoice?

b. Create and print an Aging Accounts Receivable report as of 12/15/95 and examine the QuickZoom reports for the Reid property located at 75 Sunset Road. What invoice is represented by this receivable? What was Reid Property invoiced for? What are the terms of this invoice?

c. Create and print an Aging Accounts Payable report as of 12/15/95 and examine the QuickZoom reports for Wagner & Son Painting. What bill is represented by this payable? What was Rock Castle billed for? What are the terms of this invoice?

d. Create and print an Inventory Valuation Summary as of 12/15/95 and examine the QuickZoom reports for Lk Doorknobs. Describe the two invoices in which these products were billed to customers; that is, which customers were billed, when were they billed, and so on.

trouble? Don't forget to change the Dates field to "This Fiscal Year-to-Date."

3 *Using the South-Western Home Page for More Assignments or Cases*

Go to
owen.swcollege.com

If you have Internet access, go to the home page for this textbook at owen.swcollege.com.

Select the **Chapter 1 Session 4** section, and complete the problem(s) your instructor assigns.

4 *Customizing Supporting Reports*

Customize each of the reports you created in Assignment 1 as follows on the next page:

a. Modify the Customer Balance Summary by changing the To/From dates to include amounts from September 1 through December 15, 1995. Change the columns from totals only to monthly totals. Describe the changes in customer balance over this period. Print this report.

b. Create two Accounts Receivable Aging reports, one as of 12/15/95 and one as of 11/30/95. Describe the differences in the two reports. Print both reports.

c. Create two Accounts Payable Aging reports—one one as of 12/15/95 and one as of 11/15/95. Describe the differences in the two reports. Print both reports.

d. Create two Inventory Valuation Summaries—one one as of 12/15/95 and one as of 9/30/95. Describe the differences in the two reports. Print both reports.

Session 4 Case Problem: JENNINGS & ASSOCIATES

Kelly Jennings created financial reports and submitted them to her banker to secure a loan. Today Kelly received a phone call from her banker. He told her that the balance sheet she submitted requires further explanation. He'd like to see some documentation to support her company's receivables, inventory, and payables balances.

Kelly asks you to prepare and print three supporting reports using her QuickBooks file kj01cp.qbw.

1　Open kj01cp.qbw from your Student Disk.

2　Prepare an Accounts Receivable Aging report for January 31, 1997. Print this report. Write a brief paragraph in which you explain the status of the two largest balances—that is, how old they are, what was sold, and so on.

3　Prepare an Accounts Payable Aging report for January 31, 1997. Print this report. Write a brief paragraph in which you explain the status of the two largest balances—that is, how old they are, what was purchased, and so on.

4　Prepare an Inventory Valuation Summary for January 31, 1997. Print this summary. Write a brief paragraph in which you describe the most recent purchase of film. Be sure to include the date, vendor, amount, and cost per unit.

2

Setting Up Your Business's Accounting System

In this chapter you will:

- Create a new company file
- Add a new customer to the customer list
- Add a new vendor to the vendor list
- Add a new employee to the employee list
- Add a new account to the chart of accounts
- Add two new items to the item list

CASE: PHOENIX SYSTEMS CONSULTING, INC.

You hear the doorbell and go to the front door. You open it and see Casey Nicks, a friend you've known since the third grade.

Casey worked his way through college helping businesses computerize their operations. After graduation he worked six years for a software development company, but he missed the type of work he did while he was going to school. So Casey made a brave decision. He decided to leave his job and do what he enjoyed doing most—start a company that would sell and service business computer systems and software. Casey decided to name his new company Phoenix Systems Consulting, Inc.

The first thing Casey did after making this decision was to write a business plan. He spent a great deal of time thinking about what his company would do, how it would be different from similar companies, what unique goods and services it could provide, and so on. His plan was so well thought out and so well written, that New Endeavors, Inc., a venture capital firm well-known for its backing of high-tech start-up companies, decided to invest $50,000 in his company.

So Casey has come to your house to ask you for help. He must establish an accounting information system, and he hopes you can help.

"I don't know much about accounting," he says. "I'm worried that I won't be able to manage the financial details of the business. I'm confused about receivables and payables, and about debits and credits; and I don't know how I'll ever be able to create reports for New Endeavors or for my customers, not to mention my own decision making."

"Don't worry," you reassure him. "I can help you create an accounting information system quickly and easily. I learned how to use QuickBooks last year. It's an accounting software package specially designed for small businesses like yours. If you buy a copy and bring it over this weekend, I'll help you set up your accounting information system."

Casey is relieved, and he says he'll see you Saturday afternoon.

CREATING A NEW COMPANY FILE

When Casey returns on Saturday you install QuickBooks on his laptop computer, and you're ready to begin. You tell him that first you must create a new company file. There are two ways to do this. One is to use QuickBooks's EasyStep Interview—a step-by-step guided series of questions that you can answer to help you choose and set up various QuickBooks features. The second way is to skip the EasyStep Interview. This way is convenient if you prefer to add minimal information to get started. Casey says that since he hasn't conducted a lot of business yet, he'd like to skip the interview.

"Skipping the interview is probably a good idea," you agree. "Besides, no matter which method you use to set up your company on QuickBooks, you can always change the decisions you make during the setup later."

If you want to know more about the EasyStep Interview, you can read the section entitled "A Word About the EasyStep Interview" at the end of this chapter. Also you can work through an entire EasyStep Interview in Case Problem 1 at the end of this chapter.

To create a new company file:

1 Before you begin, close any previously created company files.

2 Click **File**, then click **New Company**. The EasyStep Interview window appears. See Figure 2.1. Notice that there are four section tabs and the Welcome tab is selected.

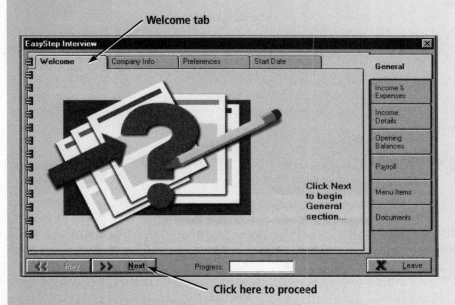

Figure 2.1
The EasyStep Interview Window

trouble? When you first launch QuickBooks, the message "Welcome to QuickBooks for Windows Version 5.0" might appear. If this occurs click the **Set up a new datafile** button.

3 Click **Next** in the EasyStep window as shown in Figure 2.1. The next Welcome screen appears. This screen asks questions about upgrading the software. Be certain that "No, I'm not upgrading" is selected.

4 Click **Next** and a screen appears titled "Setting up a new QuickBooks company." Read this screen.

Casey reads this screen, and reminds you that he wants to get started quickly. You decide to skip the interview.

To skip the EasyStep Interview:

Note: Before you proceed be sure you have time to complete all of the steps from here to page **82**.

1 Click the **Skip Interview** button. The Creating New Company window appears. See Figure 2.2. This window contains blank spaces for you to fill in information about Phoenix Systems.

Figure 2.2

Filling Out the Creating New Company Window

Fill in these three spaces

Accept these default options

Click to view a list of forms

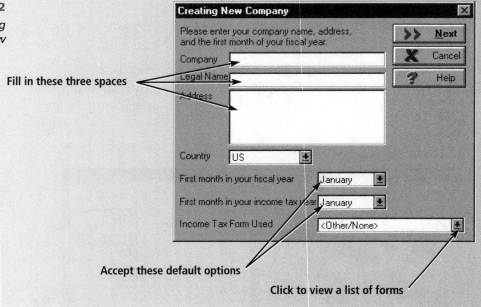

The Creating New Company window and the following screens ask for minimal information about the new company. By filling in this information you will set up Phoenix Systems quickly and begin to use QuickBooks.

To create a new company:

1 Type **Phoenix Systems** in the Company edit box.

2 Press the **Down Arrow** key once. The words Phoenix Systems automatically appear in the Legal Name edit box.

3 Press the **Right Arrow** key once, press the [**Spacebar**] once, and then type **Consulting Inc**.
trouble? If you press a key that causes this screen to disappear before you complete Step 5, click the **Prev** button, and repeat Step 3 as necessary.

4 Press the **Down Arrow** key once. Type the first line of the company's address in the Address edit box as **1234 State Street**. Press the **Enter** key. Type the second line as **Cupertino, CA 95014**.

5 The default country and the two default Januarys are correct, so press the **Down Arrow** key until the Income Tax Form Used edit box is highlighted.

6 Phoenix Systems Consulting, Inc. is a corporation. Click the **Down Arrow** on the drop-down list, and click **Form 1120 (Corporation)**.

Now you're ready to move to the next screen and select a chart of accounts.

To select a chart of accounts for a new company:

1 Click **Next** to move to the next screen. The next Creating New Company window appears. See Figure 2.3.

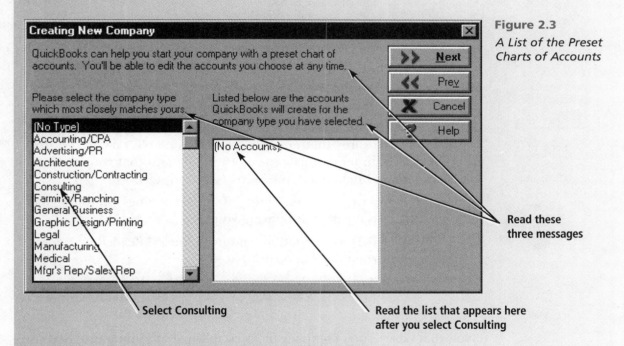

Figure 2.3
A List of the Preset Charts of Accounts

2 Read the information in this window about choosing a preset chart of accounts.

3 Select **Consulting** as the company type. Read through the account titles.

You are now ready to save your new company file, but first you must name it.

To name your new company file:

1 Click **Next**. The Filename for New Company window appears. See Figure 2.4 Notice that QuickBooks has automatically named your file phoenix_.qbw. Rename your file **myphnx02.qbw**. Save this file to a blank formatted disk in drive a:.

Figure 2.4

The Filename for New Company Window

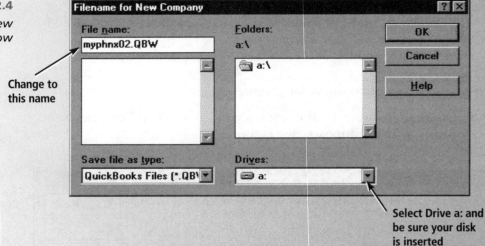

Change to
this name

Select Drive a: and
be sure your disk
is inserted

Note: Use a blank formatted "working" disk instead of your Student Disks. This insures that enough space is available on the disk for QuickBooks to temporarily store other data and that your Student Disks remain unchanged in case you need to start over.

2 Click **OK** to save your file. Messages appear letting you know that QuickBooks is creating and saving your file.

3 A Customized Documentation window appears. Read this window for your information. Then click **No**.

4 If the tips and other such windows appear, close these windows.

Now that Casey's new company file is established, it's imperative that you set certain preferences in QuickBooks to prepare for future activities. The next set of steps will establish sales tax information, provide for inventory, purchase order, and payroll use, and fix federal and state tax identification numbers.

To set preferences:

1 Click **File**, then click **Preferences**. The Preferences window appears.

2 Scroll down the Preferences icon bar, then click the **Sales Tax** icon.

3   Click **Yes**, under Do You Charge Sales Tax?

4   Click the drop-down arrow next to Most common sales tax, then click **<Add New>**, to add a new sales tax as shown in Figure 2.5.

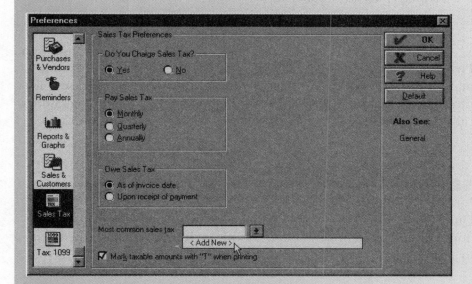

Figure 2.5
Changing Sales Tax Preferences

5   Next, a New Item window appears. Select **Sales Tax Item** from the drop-down listing of new item types. Enter **Sales Tax** as the Tax Name, **7.75%** as the Rate, and **State Board of Equalization** as the Tax Agency. Then click **OK**.

6   Click **Quick Add** in the Vendor Not Found window to add this vendor to the vendor list. Then click **OK** in the New Item window once again.

7   Next click the **Purchases & Vendors** icon from the Preferences icon bar. When the Save Changes window appears, click **Yes** to save changes in Sales Tax preferences. Then click **OK** in the Updating Sales Tax window to make all existing customers taxable and make all existing non-inventory and inventory parts taxable.

8   When the Purchases and Vendors Preferences window appears, click the check box labeled **Inventory and purchase orders are active**. Leave all other check boxes as is.

9   Scroll down the Preferences icon bar, then click the **Payroll & Employees** icon. When the Save Changes window appears, click **Yes** to save changes in Purchases & Vendor preferences.

10   When the Payroll & Employees Preferences window appears, click the option button labeled **Full payroll features**, then click **OK**.

11   An Important Payroll Notice! appears. Read this notice for your information. Then click **OK**. (Remember, the tax table used for this example is 9706.)

12 Finally, to establish the Federal and State tax identification numbers, select **Company Info** from the File menu. Then enter the Federal ID as **77-9999999**, the filing state as **CA**, and the State Employer ID as **77-9999999**.

Casey is thrilled that you have set up QuickBooks for use with Phoenix Systems. But you tell him that he still has many decisions to make and more work to do before he can use all of QuickBooks's features and generate reports. Next you need to set up what QuickBooks calls company lists.

SETTING UP COMPANY LISTS

QuickBooks uses lists to maintain information about customers, vendors, employees, items, and other significant business details. You decide to show Casey how to start creating lists for Phoenix Systems.

Customer List

A **customer list** helps expedite creating invoices, tracking receipts and balances owed, communicating with customers who have past due balances, and reporting sales by customer. Also, a customer list is necessary if customers pay at a time other than the time of sale. Casey has decided that Phoenix Systems customers will receive a standard 2% discount if they pay within 10 days of invoice. Otherwise, the balance due must be paid within 30 days. You help Casey start his customer list for Phoenix Systems by adding the first name to the list.

To add a new customer:

1 Open the file myphnx02.qbw that you recently created, if it is not already open.

2 Click **Lists,** then click **Customers:Jobs**. A blank Customer:Job List window appears.

3 Click the **Customer:Job** button and then click **New**. A New Customer window appears.

4 Fill in the New Customer window using the information provided in Figure 2.6. Note how QuickBooks duplicates appropriate information for you and that you can click the **Copy** button to copy the address from one window into the other.

5 Click the **Additional Info** tab. See Figure 2.7. Enter the information provided in this figure.

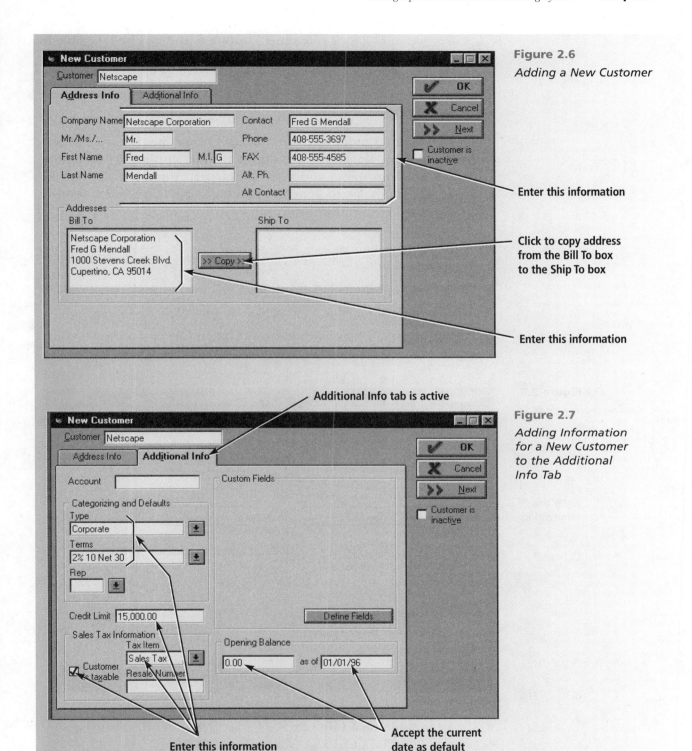

Figure 2.6
Adding a New Customer

Enter this information

Click to copy address
from the Bill To box
to the Ship To box

Enter this information

Additional Info tab is active

Figure 2.7
*Adding Information
for a New Customer
to the Additional
Info Tab*

Enter this information

Accept the current
date as default

6 If you wanted to enter additional customers at this time, you would click Next. Instead, click **OK** to accept this new customer record and close this window. The Customer:Job List window reappears, now including the customer you just added.

7 Close this window.

Casey sees how easy it is to enter customers and says he'll be able to enter the rest of his current customers on his own. So now you'll help him add a vendor.

Vendor List

In QuickBooks, a **vendor list** helps managers expedite payments to vendors or suppliers, track bills and payments due, and report by vendor expenses, amounts owed, and items purchased. You tell Casey that he can use his vendor list to generate purchase orders, record inventory shipments, and pay vendor invoices.

To add a new vendor:

1 Click **Lists**, and then click **Vendors**. A Vendor List window appears.

2 Click **Vendor**, then click **New**. A New Vendor window appears.

3 Fill in the New Vendor window using the information provided in Figure 2.8.

Figure 2.8
Adding a New Vendor

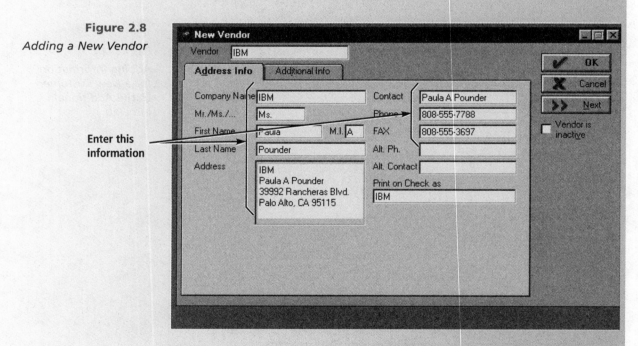

4 Click the **Additional Info** tab. See Figure 2.9. Enter the information provided in this figure.

5 If you wanted to enter additional vendors at this time, you would click Next. Instead click **OK** to record and close this window. The Vendor window appears, which now includes the vendor you just added.

6 Close this window.

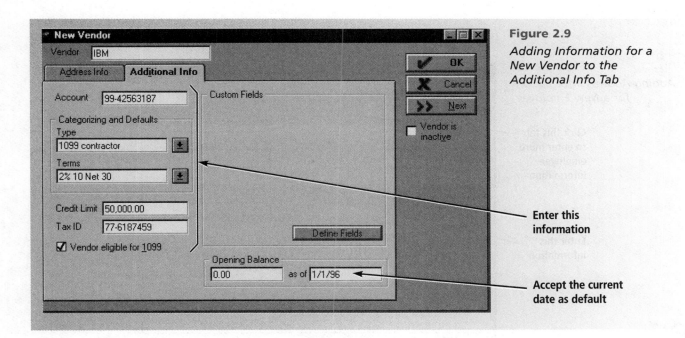

Figure 2.9

Adding Information for a New Vendor to the Additional Info Tab

As with the customer list, Casey is pleased with how easily you added the vendor to the vendor list. You tell him that the employee list is next.

Employee List

QuickBooks can accommodate a lot of information about employees in an **employee list**. You know that for the time being Casey plans to have only three employees—himself and two people he worked with at his last job. For now, you decide to enter minimal employee information that will allow Casey to print each employee's name and address on payroll checks, track payroll expenses and withholdings, and track sales revenue generated by each employee.

To add a new employee:

1 Click **Lists**, then click **Employees**. A blank Employee List window appears.

2 Click **Employees**, then click **New**. A New Employee window appears.

3 Be certain that the Address Info tab is selected. Then fill in the blank spaces on this tab using the information in Figure 2.10.

4 Click the **Payroll Info** tab. Fill in the blank spaces on this tab as shown in Figure 2.11.

5 Click **Taxes**. The Taxes window appears.

Figure 2.10
*Adding Address Information
for a New Employee*

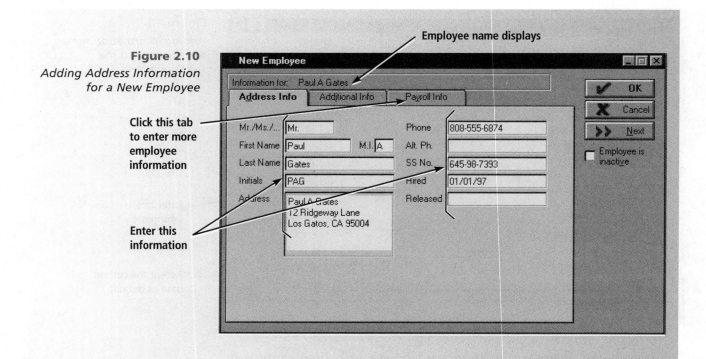

Figure 2.11
*Adding Payroll Information
for Paul Gates*

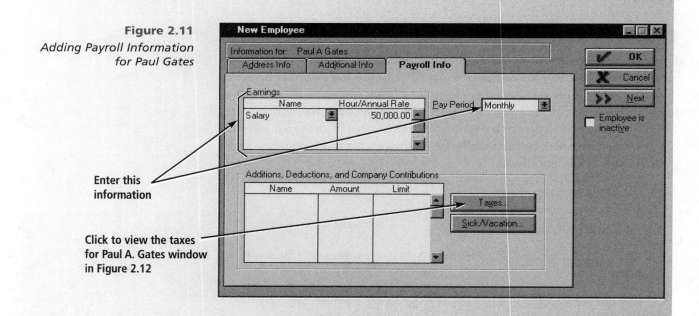

6 Complete the federal taxes for the Paul Gates window using the information in Figure 2.12. Then click **OK** to accept this information and return to the Payroll Info tab.

trouble? Be sure all tax check boxes are checked and set the filing status to Married.

Click to view other Filing Status choices

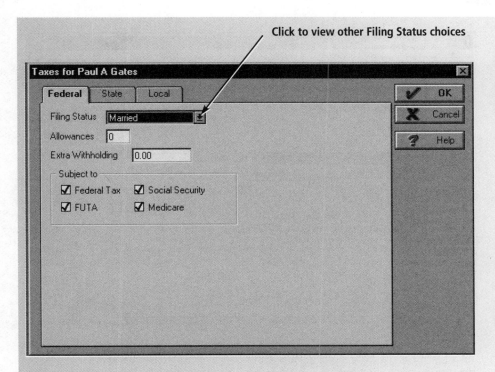

Figure 2.12
*Adding Federal Tax
Information for
Paul Gates*

7 Click the **State** tab.

8 Complete the state taxes information provided in Figure 2.13. When you select **CA** as the filing state for State Unemployment, QuickBooks prompts you with a Payroll Item Not Found window. Click the **Set Up** button.

9 The New State Unemployment Payroll Item window appears. Accept the given information and enter **EDD (Employment Development Department)** in the Payable To edit box. Then click **OK**.

10 The EDD is not currently a vendor, thus a Vendor Not Found window appears. Click **QuickAdd** to enter this new vendor.

11 Then click **3%** in the Rate % edit box and click **OK**.

12 A warning screen may appear if the State Employer ID# is missing from Company Information. Please add the ID# and click **OK** to return to the Company Information screen.

13 A FUTA Credit window appears. Often a state may be allowed credit towards federal unemployment tax (FUTA) for state unemployment tax contributions. Click **Yes**.

14 Select **CA** as the filing state for State Disability in the edit box.

15 This payroll item is not found either and thus you must click **Set Up**.

16 A New State Disability Payroll Item window appears. Enter **EDD** in the Payable To edit box.

Figure 2.13

Adding State Tax Information for Paul Gates

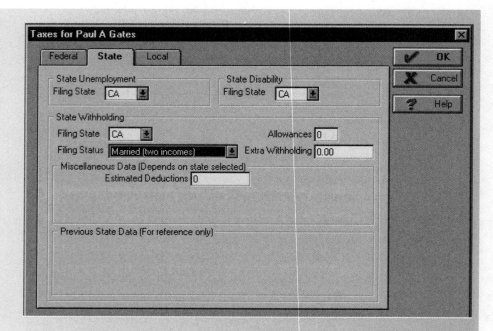

17 Now select **CA** as the filing state for State Withholding.

18 This payroll item is not found either and thus you must click **Set Up**.

19 A New State Withholding Payroll Item window appears. Enter **EDD** in the Payable To edit box, then click **OK**.

20 Then click **OK** to accept this information and return to the Payroll Info tab.

21 Click **OK** to record and close this window. If you wanted to enter additional employees at this time you would click Next instead.

22 Click **Leave As Is** in the New Employee: Payroll Info window which appears. The Employee List window reappears. Note that now it includes Paul Gates.

23 Close this window.

The next list you want to show Casey is the chart of accounts.

Chart of Accounts

You know from your accounting course that a **chart of accounts** provides the structure of a financial reporting system. QuickBooks provides several preset charts of accounts.

"But we already created a chart of accounts when we set up the company," Casey protests. "We selected the 'Consulting' preset chart of accounts."

"Yes," you agree, "but that chart of accounts does not contain cash, accounts receivable, inventory, or accounts payable accounts."

Casey looks puzzled. "I'm sure I'll need those accounts for Phoenix Systems," he says, "so why did we pick 'Consulting'?"

"We picked 'Consulting' because it is the correct choice," you explain. "We need to modify the chart of accounts and the EasyStep Interview wouldn't have allowed us to do that."

To modify a chart of accounts:

1 Click **Accnt** on the icon bar. See Figure 2.14. (Alternatively, you could click **Lists**, then click **Chart of Accounts**.) The account titles in the preset Consulting chart of accounts appears. Look down this list to familiarize yourself with the titles.

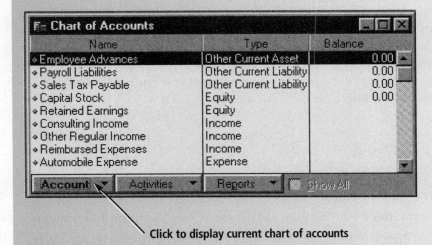

Figure 2.14
Phoenix Systems Chart of Accounts

Click to display current chart of accounts

2 Click **Account**, then click **New**. A New Account window appears.

3 Fill in the New Account window using the information in Figure 2.15.

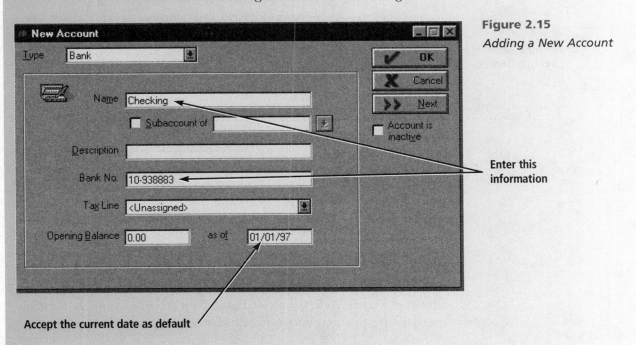

Figure 2.15
Adding a New Account

Enter this information

Accept the current date as default

4 Click **OK** to add the account. The Chart of Accounts window appears. Note that it now includes the new account you just added. (If you had wanted to enter additional accounts, you would have clicked Next instead.)

5 Close this window.

Item List

Item lists expedite the recording and reporting of sales activities. An item can be a service performed, such as computer installation or maintenance; or it can be an inventory part, such as a hard disk or monitor. You tell Casey that he can use the information in item lists to help generate purchase orders and customer invoices as well as to manage inventory receipts. He suggests that you enter two new items— one is a service and one is an item of inventory.

To add a new item:

1 Click **Item** on the icon bar. (Alternatively, you could click **Lists**, and then click **Items**.) An item list appears.

2 Click the **Item** button, then click **New**. A New Item window appears.

3 Fill in the New Item window using the information in Figure 2.16. Enter **Maintenance & Repair Revenue** in the Account box.

Click arrow to verify types of items

Figure 2.16

Entering a New Service Item

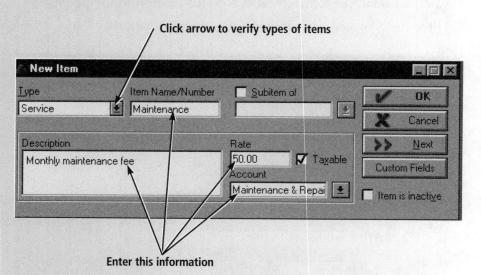

Enter this information

When you type **Maintenance & Repairs Revenue** in the Account box and click **OK**, an Account Not Found error message will appear, as shown in Figure 2.17. Click **Set Up**. A New Account window appears recognizing this new account as an Income type account.

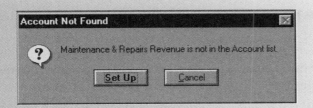

Figure 2.17
*Error Message for
an Account that
Does Not Exist*

trouble? Note that QuickBooks uses the word "income" to describe what most accountants refer to as "revenue." Unfortunately, there is no way to alter this word whenever QuickBooks uses it. But you can, if you wish, change the titles of the accounts themselves to "consulting revenues," "parts revenues," and so on.

4 Click **OK** to enter this new account.

5 Click the **Item** button and then click **New**. A New Item window appears.

6 Fill in the New Item window using the information in Figure 2.18. When you type **Computer Sales** in the Income Account box and then click **OK**, an Account Not Found error message will appear. Click **Set Up**. A New Account window appears recognizing this new account as an Income (that is, a revenue) type account.

Click to view other item types

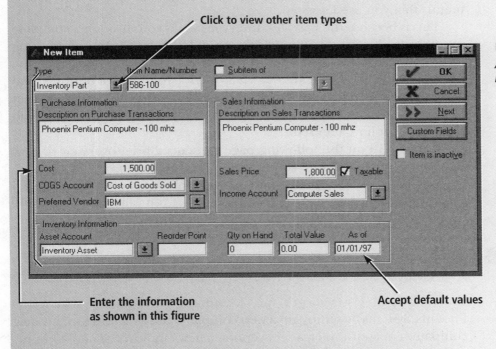

Figure 2.18
*Adding a New
Inventory Item*

Enter the information
as shown in this figure

Accept default values

trouble? You might think that this New Item window would be identical to the previous window. But when you change the type from Service to Inventory Part, the New Item window changes its format. If you haven't done so already, click the **Down Arrow** in the Type box and click **Inventory Part** in the New Item window.

7 Click **OK** to enter this new account.

8 Click **OK** to close this window. If you had wanted to enter additional items at this time, you would have clicked Next instead.

9 The Item List window appears, now including the two items you just added. While the list window is active click **Print List** from the File menu.

10 Close this window.

A WORD ABOUT THE EASYSTEP INTERVIEW

At the beginning of this session, you skipped the EasyStep Interview to create Phoenix Systems. This was because the purpose of this text is to acquaint you with QuickBooks in the simplest and most efficient way. But if you were really setting up your own company, Intuit Inc. recommends that you use EasyStep.

This is because the EasyStep Interview walks you through a complete set up procedure and eliminates the need to deal with your accounting information system "on the fly." Also EasyStep helps you determine the best way to use all of QuickBooks's features for your type of business, and it automatically creates some of the QuickBooks accounts and items that you need. You can exit the interview at any time, and QuickBooks will save what you have entered.

Figure 2.19 on the following page presents a brief overview of how EasyStep is organized into seven sections and four tabs.

You will have an opportunity to work through an entire EasyStep Interview with a complete set of company data if you work Case Problem 1 for Jennings & Associates at the end of this chapter.

END NOTE

You've helped Casey begin the accounting information system for Phoenix Systems by setting up a new company, and by adding to this new company a new customer, a new vendor, a new employee, a new account, and two new items. You tell Casey that he can now begin recording Phoenix System's first business transactions. Casey is delighted with how easy QuickBooks has been to use, and he says he'll come back tomorrow with the details of Phoenix's first transactions.

Figure 2.19 *An Overview of the EasyStep Interview*

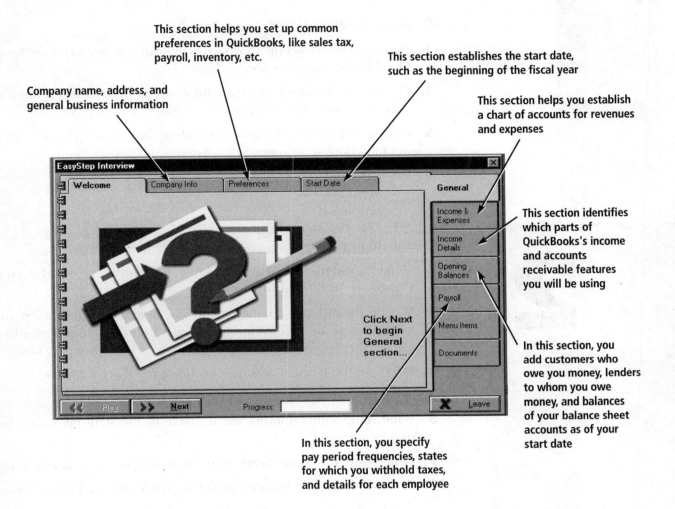

This section helps you set up common preferences in QuickBooks, like sales tax, payroll, inventory, etc.

This section establishes the start date, such as the beginning of the fiscal year

Company name, address, and general business information

This section helps you establish a chart of accounts for revenues and expenses

This section identifies which parts of QuickBooks's income and accounts receivable features you will be using

Click Next to begin General section...

In this section, you add customers who owe you money, lenders to whom you owe money, and balances of your balance sheet accounts as of your start date

In this section, you specify pay period frequencies, states for which you withhold taxes, and details for each employee

practice

chapter

2

Chapter 2 Questions

1 Describe the two set-up approaches that you can use to create a new QuickBooks company file.

2 How do you know when to use the EasyStep Interview and when to skip the Interview?

3 In your own words, explain what each of the following terms means in QuickBooks:

    a. Customer
    b. Vendor
    c. Employee
    d. Chart of accounts
    e. Item

4 What payment terms are available to customers on the New Customer Additional Info tab?

5 What is the difference between a service item and an inventory part item? How is the window for adding new items different depending on whether you are adding a service item or inventory part item?

6 What are the types of accounts in the chart of accounts list?

7 What federal taxes might an employee be subject to?

8 What filing status options are available in the state tax set-up for new employees?

9 What pay period options are available in the payroll set-up window?

10 Describe how accounts can be set up while entering information into a list.

Chapter 2 Assignments

1 *Adding More Information to Phoenix Systems Consulting, Inc.*

Use phnx02cp.qbw from your Student Disk.

    a. Add the following new customers:

        Customer: Los Gatos School District
        Contact: Mr. Francis L. Cahn
        Address: 1000 Apple Farm Rd., Los Gatos, CA 95110
        Phone: 408-555-9788
        Type: Corporate
        Terms: Net 30
        Rep: PAG
        Credit limit: 10,000
        Customer is taxable: Yes
        Tax item: Sales tax

Customer: Jdesign
Contact: Mr. John F. Gomez
Address: 235 Ridgefield Place, Fremont, CA 95110
Phone: 408-555-3483
Type: Corporate
Terms: 2% 10 net 30
Rep: PAG
Credit limit: 5,000
Customer is taxable: Yes
Tax item: Sales tax

b. Add the following new vendors:

Vendor: Apple Computer, Inc.
Contact: Mr. Barry G. Franks
Address: One Corporate Way, Cupertino, CA 95110
Phone: 408-555-9787
Account: 94-6856-0122
Type: Manufacturer
Terms: Due on receipt
Credit limit: 3,000
Tax ID: 77-6841257
Vendor eligible for 1099: Yes

Vendor: Bengal Drives, Inc.
Contact: Ms. Kelly Sweenie
Address: 4500 Rucker Rd., Santa Barbara, CA 93103
Phone: 805-555-8777
Account: 16-11123
Type: Manufacturer
Terms: 2% 10 net 30
Credit limit: 8,000
Tax ID: 77-1487125
Vendor eligible for 1099: No

c. Add the following new employees. Select the Leave As Is option when prompted for Local/Taxes and Sick/Vacation.

Employee: Mr. Casey K. Nicks
Address: 345 Ocean View Dr., Santa Cruz, CA 95888
Phone: 408-555-1287
SS No: 566-79-3511
Hired: 1/1/96
Pay period: Monthly
Yearly salary: 60,000
Filing status: Married, filing jointly
Subject to: Federal tax, state tax, Social Security, FUTA, and Medicare
Filing state: CA

Employee: Ms. Kylie W. Patrick
Address: 10101 Wildway, San Jose, CA 95822
Phone: 408-555-3050

SS No: 426-85-6974
Hired: 1/1/96
Pay period: Monthly
Yearly salary: 40,000
Filing status: Head of household
Subject to: Federal tax, state tax, Social Security, FUTA, and Medicare
Filing state: CA

d. Add the following new accounts:

Type: Income
Name: Computer Add-ons

Type: Long-Term Liability
Name: Long-Term Debt

e. Add the following new items:

Type: Inventory Part
Item name: 800mb HD
Description: 800mb Bengal Hard Disk
Cost: 250.00
COGS account: Cost of Goods Sold
Preferred Vendor: Bengal Drives
Asset Account: Inventory Asset
Sales Price: 300.00
Income Account: Computer Add-ons

Type: Inventory Part
Item name: 1 gig HD
Description: 1,000mb Bengal Hard Disk
Cost: 450.00
COGS account: Cost of Goods Sold
Preferred Vendor: Bengal Drives
Asset Account: Inventory Asset
Sales Price: 550.00
Income Account: Computer Add-ons

Type: Service
Item name: Installation
Description: Installation of computer add-ons
Rate: 45.00
Account: Maintenance & Repairs

f. Print an updated copy of each list modified above.

2   *Creating a New Company: Nashua AutoMarket*

a. Create a new company by skipping the EasyStep Interview. Use the following information:

Name: Nashua AutoMarket
Address: 555 Liberty Lane, Reno, NV 89557
Fiscal year begins: January
No sales tax

Federal ID: 77-1233220
State: NV
State Employer ID: 77-3325099

Select a retail chart of accounts and create your own answers to any other questions asked in the set-up process. Save this file with the default file name provided by QuickBooks on a separate disk.

b. Add a new customer to the Nashua AutoMarket file:

Name: Diaz-Cruz Automotive
Billing and Shipping address: 9396 Maryland Lane,
⠀⠀⠀⠀⠀⠀⠀⠀⠀⠀⠀⠀⠀⠀⠀⠀⠀⠀Pensacola, FL 99999
Create your own phone numbers, contacts, credit limit, and terms.

c. Add a new vendor to the Nashua AutoMarket file:

Name: Missoula Auto Supply
Address: 2231 Hawk Rd., Billings, MT 99999

Create your own phone numbers, contacts, credit limit, and terms.

d. Add a new employee to the Nashua AutoMarket file:

Name: William P. Biaggi
Address: 2023 Lane, Reno, NV 99999
Create your own phone numbers, Social Security number, and hired date.
Pay period: Monthly
Yearly salary: $22,000
Taxes: Subject to all federal taxes
Filing status: Single

e. Add a new account to the Nashua AutoMarket file:

Type: Income
Name: Product Sales

f. Add a new item to the Nashua AutoMarket file:

Name: Bumper 100
Description: Blazer Bumper 1996
Type: Inventory part
Income Account: Product sales
On hand: 0
Cost: $300.00
Sales price: 400.00

g. Print a copy of each list created above.

3 *Using the South-Western Home Page for More Assignments or Cases*

If you have Internet access, go to the home page for this textbook at owen.swcollege.com.

⠀⠀Select the **Chapter 2** section, and complete the problem(s) your instructor assigns.

Go to
owen.swcollege.com

http://

Chapter 2 Case Problem 1: JENNINGS & ASSOCIATES—The EasyStep Interview

You saw in Chapter 1 that Kelly Jennings produced a balance sheet, an income statement, and supporting reports (as of January 31, 1997) for her banker. Unfortunately, the QuickBooks file that Kelly used to store these financial reports was destroyed by a nasty virus, and Kelly failed to make backup files to avoid loss of data! So she must now recreate her file. This time, Kelly wants you to help her recreate her company file using EasyStep.

Use the following information to create a new file for Kelly Jennings. This information is presented to correspond to the seven sections of the interview. When you encounter interview questions for which answers are not provided in this problem, make up your own answers. The purpose of this problem is to give you experience using the EasyStep Interview, so focus on the interview itself.

You may pause at any point in the interview and return later to complete it. Be sure to save this file often as you create it. Name it mykelly1.qbw.

1 *General*

The company name is Jennings & Associates. It is located at 1200 Constellation Rd. Suite E, San Martin, CA 93107. Its federal tax ID is 77-9999999. Kelly began using QuickBooks on January 1, 1997; the fiscal year-end is December 31. The company is an advertising/public relations corporation and files a Form 1120 for federal taxes. Jennings & Associates inventories photograph film and wants to use QuickBooks's inventory capabilities. The company collects sales taxes at the rate of 7.75%, which it then remits to the State Board of Equalization. It has three employees. Kelly wants to use a service-oriented invoice form and QuickBooks's payroll feature.

Kelly has decided, for the time being, not to give customers written estimates, but she does want to track employee time on each job. She's decided to track and record reimbursable expenses as both income and expense. She does not want to use QuickBooks's classification feature, but she does want bills entered upon their receipt, even though she will not pay them until a later due date. She prefers to view the reminder list only by request. Finally, she's told you to start using QuickBooks as of January 1, 1997.

Although Kelly wants you to start using QuickBooks for 1997 transactions as of 1/1/97, it's essential that you specify a start date of 12/31/96. This is because of how the QuickBooks software treats net income.

2 *Income and Expenses*

Jennings & Associates never receives payment at the time a service is provided. They invoice each client as they provide services. The service items provided by QuickBooks for an advertising/ public relations firm will be adequate for their current needs. There is no need for non-inventory items or other charges at this point.

The firm does charge for film costs incurred, and they use the inventory tools provided in QuickBooks to manage film purchases. Two types of film are inventoried. The first, regular grade film, costs $4.45 per roll and is normally purchased from Rex's Film Supply located at 800 North Central, Suite F, San Martin, CA 93017. The cost of the film is included in an inventory asset account until it is sold. When sold, the film cost is charged to an expense account (film expenses) and a revenue account (fee income:film) is recorded at the price of $7.50 per roll. A second grade of film (high quality) is also purchased from Rex's and costs $15.00 per roll. The same accounting rules as used for regular film are followed except the sales price of the film is $25.00 per roll. (*Note*: All film is taxable.)

3   *Opening Balances*

Although Jennings & Associates will begin using QuickBooks 1/1/97, customer, vendor, and other account balances existed as of 12/31/96. Table 2.1 shows which customers owe Jennings & Associates as of 12/31/96.

Table 2.2 shows vendors with whom Jennings & Associates did business during 1996.

Jennings & Associates had two checking accounts, one at Union Bank with a balance of $2,590 on December 31, 1996 and one at First Valley Savings and Loan with a balance of $1,000 as of December 31, 1996. The firm owned computer equipment with an original cost of $4,000 and accumulated depreciation of $1,000, and furniture with an original cost of $2,500 and accumulated depreciation of $500 on December 31, 1996. Lastly, they owed $5,000 to the Bank of San Martin due and payable on December 31, 1998.

4   *Payroll*

Jennings & Associates' state employer ID is 77-1234567. Kelly pays her employees semi-monthly. The state (CA) unemployment tax rate is 3% payable to the EDD, and the company pays the full FUTA rate of 6.2% payable to the IRS. Kelly is salaried and her employees are paid hourly. All are subject to federal income, Social Security, Medicare, and FUTA taxes. Currently, Kelly does not use QuickBooks to track and document sick and vacation time.

Table 2.3 shows Jennings & Associates employees of 1/1/97. As of January 1, 1997 Jennings & Associates has paid all salaries and taxes owed. Thus, it does not have any payroll tax liabilities carried over from prior years.

Customer	Address	Amount
AAA Appliance	Attn: Jane E. Seymor 1034 Sycamore San Martin, CA 93110	$350
Big 10 Sporting Goods	Attn: Sammy A. Goodwin 1003 A Street San Martin, CA 93100	$250
Bob and Mary Schultz	Bob and Mary Schultz 122 Garden Street San Martin, CA 93107	$500
Ray's Chevron	Attn: Fanny J. May 1990 Broadway San Martin, CA 93110	$150
Sally's Fabrics	Attn: Ray E. Farray 900 West Laurel San Martin, CA 93115	$200
Fancy Yogurt	Attn: Paul F. Montoya 3299 Bonita Lane San Martin, CA 93107	$500
Paulsons Nursery	Attn: Robert J. Paulson 100 Central San Martin, CA 93110	$600
Evelyn Walker Real Estate	Attn: Nancy P. Revlon 3233 Central San Martin, CA 93107	$700

Vendor	Address	Terms	Amount Owed
Frank Mendez Properties	Attn: Frank Mendez 12400 Calle Real San Martin, CA 93110	Net 15	$700
Banks Office Supply	Attn: Pamela Reese 1209 Oak Lane San Martin, CA 93110	Net 30	$0
On-Time Copy Shop	Attn: Mrs. Jennifer Jacobs 3402 A Street San Martin, CA 93110	Net 30	$125
So. Cal Gas	Attn: Kyle N. Schultz 200 South Main San Martin, CA 93110	Net 30	$65
Pacific Electric Company	12000 North Main San Martin, CA 93110	Net 30	$35
General Telephone	12100 North Main San Martin, CA 93110	Net 30	$75

Name	Address	SS#	Hired	Salary	Status	Table 2.3
Kelly Jennings	2333 Dire Straits Rd. San Martin, CA 93107	854-60-7882	12/1/96	$48,000	Head of house-hold	*Jennings & Associates Employees as of 1/1/97*
Diane Murphy	455 Galaxy Rd. San Martin, CA 93107	556-89-9999	12/1/96	$15/hr	Married filing jointly	
Cheryl A. Boudreau	19090 Mockingbird Ln. San Martin, CA 93107	545-99-5512	12/15/96	$15/hr	Single	

5 *Assignment*

Print the following as of January 1, 1997:

Standard balance sheet
Customer list
Vendor list
Item list
Employee list
Chart of accounts

Chapter 2 Case Problem 2: JENNINGS & ASSOCIATES—Skipping the EasyStep Interview

Kelly wants you to help her recreate her company file without using the EasyStep Interview. Use the same information from above to create a file for Kelly Jennings. Name this file mykelly2.qbw.

1 *Assignment*

Print the following as of January 1, 1997:

Standard balance sheet
Customer list
Vendor list
Item list
Employee list
Chart of accounts

Cash-Oriented Business Activities

In this chapter you will:

- Record cash-oriented transactions classified as financing activities, such as owner contributions

- Record cash-oriented transactions classified as investing activities, such as equipment purchases

- Record cash-oriented transactions classified as operating activities, such as inventory purchases and sales

CASE: PHOENIX SYSTEMS CONSULTING, INC.

Three months have passed since Casey first appeared at your door asking for help, and Phoenix Systems has been growing quickly—so quickly, in fact, that Casey has decided to hire a full-time accountant. With your help, Casey has entered all of Phoenix's business transactions to date into QuickBooks. Now Casey has asked you to train his new accountant—Karen Yamamoto—who recently graduated from college with a degree in accounting. You agree to begin training Karen next week.

When you meet Karen, she confesses that this is her first full-time job, and she's a little nervous.

"Relax!" you say, trying to reassure her. "QuickBooks is very easy for first-time users to learn, and you'll be delighted with how much it will help you do your job."

"The best way to learn QuickBooks is to jump right in," you add. "As Casey probably told you, Phoenix's first quarter—January 1 through March 31—has just ended. I know he's already entered all of the transactions for the first quarter into the company's QuickBooks file. So I thought we should begin by reviewing some of Phoenix's first quarter transactions. Then you can practice entering transactions into a temporary file to see what it's like to use QuickBooks."

Karen suggests that you can give her a complete overview of QuickBooks's capabilities if you show her Phoenix's transactions organized by the three fundamental business activities—financing, investing, and operating. She explains that **financing activities** are initiated when money or other resources are obtained from short-term nontrade creditors, long-term creditors, and owners. Financing activities are completed when amounts owed are repaid to or otherwise settled with these same creditors and owners. She explains further that **investing activities** are initiated when the money obtained from financing activities is applied to non-operating uses, such as buying investment securities and productive equipment. Investing activities are completed when the investment securities or productive equipment are sold. Finally, **operating activities** occur when the money obtained from financing activities and the long-term assets obtained from investing activities are applied either to purchase or to produce goods and services for sale. Operating activities are substantially completed when goods are delivered or sold and when services are performed.

"Wow, they taught you well in college!" you exclaim. "Let's get started with a few of Phoenix's cash-oriented financing activities."

RECORDING CASH-ORIENTED FINANCING ACTIVITIES

You begin with two financing activities. The first occurred on January 2, 1997, when Casey contributed $25,000 to start the business.

To record Casey's deposit:

1 Copy phnx03.qbw from your Student Disk to your working disk. See "Your Student Disks" in Chapter 1 if you need more information.

2 Open phnx03.qbw from your working disk.

3 Click **Activities** and then click **Make Deposits**. The Make Deposits window appears. Note that QuickBooks has automatically inserted today's date.

4 Enter the information for Casey's contribution as shown in Figure 3.1. Be sure to enter the correct date. Notice that QuickBooks speeds up data entry by providing drop-down lists and by recognizing and filling in names that Casey has already entered into the Phoenix file.

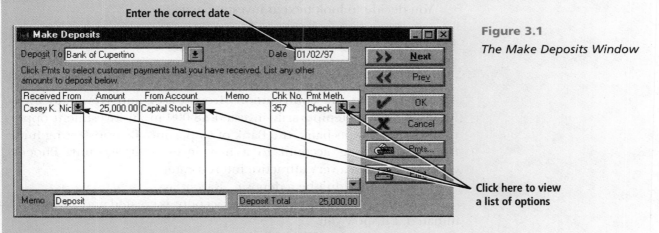

Figure 3.1
The Make Deposits Window

5 Click **Next** to record the deposit.

The second deposit was made on January 10, 1997, when New Endeavors—the venture capital company that invested in Phoenix Systems—contributed $50,000.

To record New Endeavors' deposit:

1 Type **New Endeavors** in the Received From edit box of the Make Deposits window.

2 Click in the **Amount** edit box.

3 Click **Set Up** in the Name Not Found window.

4 Click **Other** in the Select Name Type window, then click **OK**.

5 Enter the information for New Endeavors in the New Name window as shown in Figure 3.2, then click **OK**.

6 Enter the date of the deposit—**January 10, 1997**—and amount—**50,000**—and the account—**Capital Stock**—in the Make Deposits window. Then click **OK** to close the Make Deposits window.

Figure 3.2
*The New Name
Window*

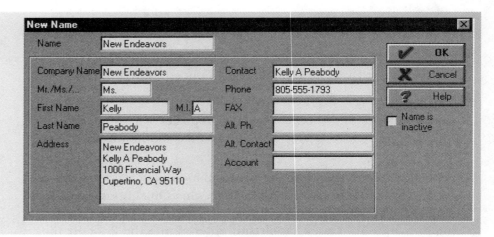

You decide to look next at investing activities.

RECORDING CASH-ORIENTED INVESTING ACTIVITIES

After depositing the contributions from Casey and New Endeavors, Phoenix Systems temporarily invested $8,000 in an investment opportunity offered by its bank, the Bank of Cupertino. By transferring funds from its checking account to a new investment account, Phoenix expected to earn a very attractive interest rate.

"But that wouldn't be a deposit," Karen says.

"You're right," you agree. "A new account is created and a transfer is initiated. I'll show you."

To create a new account and record a transfer of funds:

1 Click **Accnt** on the icon bar.

2 Click the **Account** button then click **New**. A New Account window appears.

3 Enter **Bank** in the Type box, if it is not already, there and **Short-term Investments** in the Name box, then click **OK**.

4 With the Short-term Investments account name selected, click **Activities**, then click **Use Register**.

5 Enter the information shown in Figure 3.3 to record the deposit. Begin by entering the deposit amount of **8,000.00** on the first line. Next, select **Bank of Cupertino** on the second line and **Transfer** in Memo. Then click **Record**.

Figure 3.3
*The Short-Term
Investments Register*

Date	Number	Payee		Payment	✓	Deposit	Balance
	Type	Account	Memo				
01/10/97	Number	Payee		Payment		8,000.00	
	TRANSFR	Bank of Cupertino	Transfer				

TRANSFR automatically appears when you enter a deposit amount here

6 Close the Short-term Investments register.

7 Close the Chart of Accounts window.

Phoenix also had other investment activity over the last few months, and you want to walk Karen through two more transactions. Both transactions represent checks that were written from the Bank of Cupertino checking account. The first check represents the purchase of a computer used in the business.

To write a check to purchase equipment:

1 Click **Check** on the icon bar.

2 Click **Bank of Cupertino** as the bank account from the drop-down list, if it is not already there.

   trouble? Be sure to select Bank of Cupertino as the bank account from which this check is written. The default account is the last one used, which in this case might be the Short-term Investments account.

3 Press the **Tab** key two times to accept the check number provided by QuickBooks.

   trouble? The check number specified on your check is dependent on what order you entered the information in this and other chapters. Do not worry if your check number is different from the check number shown in Figure 3.4 on the following page.

4 Type **2/3/97** as the date, then press the **Tab** key.

5 Type **Office Mart** as the payee, then press the **Tab** key. Note that since Office Mart is a new name, QuickBooks requires more information for this new vendor.

6 Click **Set up** in the Name Not Found window.

7 Click **Vendor**, if necessary, in the Select Name Type window, then click **OK**.

8 Type **Office Mart** as the Company Name in the New Vendor window, then type **2900 Fair Ct. [Enter] Cupertino, CA 95110** as the address for Office Mart in the Address edit box, then click **OK**.

9 Type **6750** as the amount, then press the **Tab** key 3 times to move the cursor to the Account field.

   trouble? Near the bottom of the Write Checks window are two tabs—one labeled Expenses and one labeled Items. The Expenses label is somewhat misleading because you can type or select any account to appear here, including assets. On the other hand, you use the Items tab to enter inventory acquisitions only. Click on either the Expenses tab or the Items tab accordingly.

10 Type **Computer Equipment** in the Account field as shown in Figure 3.4.

Figure 3.4

Writing a Check to Purchase Equipment

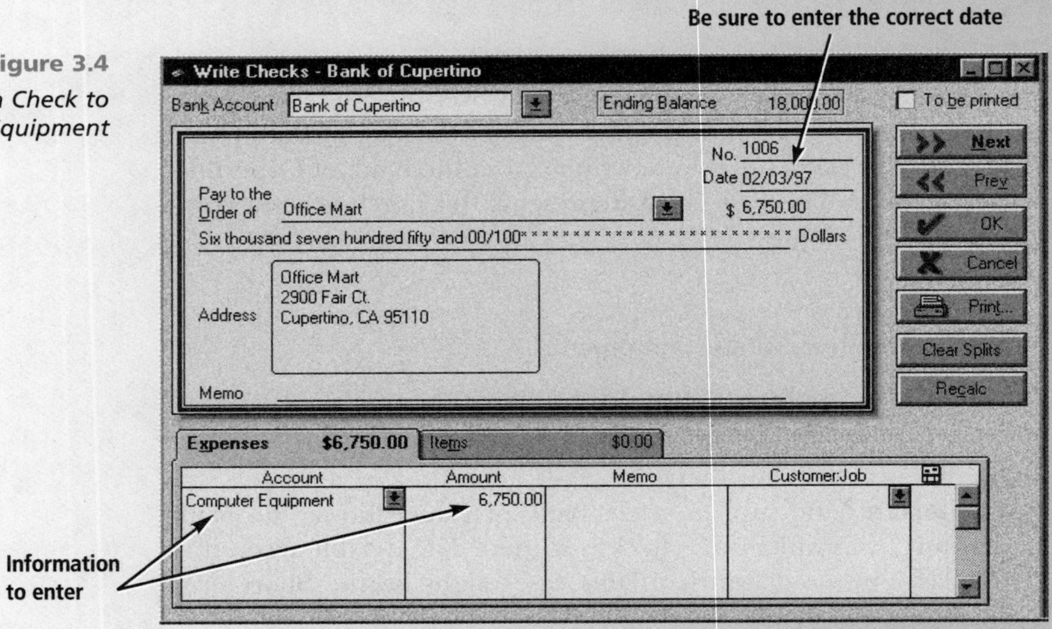

Be sure to enter the correct date

Information to enter

11 Press the **Tab** key, then click the **Set Up** button in the Account Not Found window that appears.

12 Change the Type to **Fixed Asset**, then click **OK**. QuickBooks recommends that all fixed asset accounts have a separate cost and accumulated depreciation account as subaccounts to the main classification.

13 To set up individual cost and accumulated depreciation accounts click **Acct** on the toolbar.

14 Click the **Account** button, then click **New**.

15 Change the Type to **Fixed Asset**, and the Name to **Cost**.

16 Click the check box next to Subaccount of, select **Computer Equipment** from the drop-down list, then click **Next**.

17 Follow the same steps to create an Accumulated Depreciation account as a subaccount of Computer Equipment. Then click **OK**.

18 Change the name of the account for this check from "Computer Equipment" to "Computer Equipment: Cost."

19 If necessary, click the **To be printed** check box to make sure it is *not* checked.

20 Click **Next** to record this check.

The second check you want to show Karen is for the purchase of a short-term investment—Casey has decided to use some of Phoenix's funds to invest in mutual funds.

To write a check to purchase mutual funds, as a short-term investment:

1 Be certain that Bank of Cupertino is still selected as the Bank Account.

2 Type **Sky Investments** as the payee.

3 Press the **Tab** key once. Note that since Sky Investments is a new name, QuickBooks requires more information.

4 Click **Set up** in the Name Not Found window.

5 Click **Other** in the Select Name Type window, then click **OK**.

6 Type **Sky Investments** as the Company Name in the New Vendor window, then type **Paul R Getty [Enter] 9347 Piedmont [Enter] Cupertino, CA 95110 [Enter] 408-555-9741** in the New Name window, then click **OK**.

7 Enter the additional information for the check to Sky Investments as shown in Figure 3.5. Note that the account type—Investments, an Other Current Asset Account—needs to be set up at this time as well.

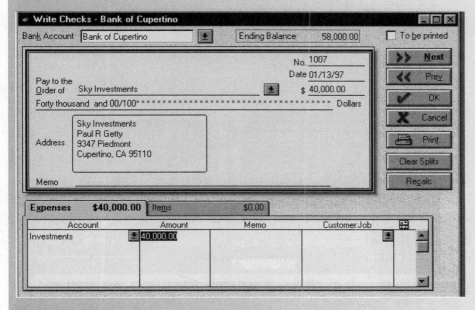

Figure 3.5

Writing a Check to Purchase an Investment

8 Click **OK** to record this check.

You're now ready to record the last type of fundamental business activity—operating activities.

RECORDING CASH-ORIENTED OPERATING ACTIVITIES

You tell Karen that Phoenix uses purchase orders to help manage its business activities. She remarks that, typically, purchase orders have no impact on financial statements. But you quickly point out that purchase orders are an important control feature in QuickBooks and so she should practice using them.

You decide to pull purchase order PO 3001 from the company's files and have Karen use it as a sample to practice creating a purchase order.

To create a purchase order:

1 Click the **PO** button on the icon bar.

2 Enter the information shown in Figure 3.6 up to the Item column.

Be certain this date is correct   Start with 3001

Figure 3.6
*Creating a
Purchase Order*

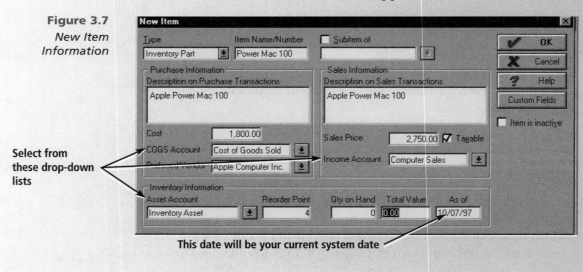

3 Type **Power Mac 100** as the item to be purchased. This is a new item, and so additional information is required.

4 Click **Set Up** to create a new item. The New Item window appears.

5 Enter the information shown in Figure 3.7, then click **OK**. The Create Purchase Orders window reappears.

Figure 3.7
*New Item
Information*

Select from
these drop-down
lists

This date will be your current system date

6 Type **5** in the Qty (Quantity) space, then click **OK** in the Create Purchase Orders window.

Phoenix uses purchase orders for ordering products, as well as for receiving products. For example, Purchase Order 3001 was actually filled a few days after it was sent. As soon as Phoenix received this inventory, a check was generated to pay the bill. Phoenix is a relatively young company, so many vendors require payment on delivery. You show Karen how QuickBooks records this receipt of inventory and vendor payment.

To record the receipt and payment of inventory ordered:

1 Click the **Check** button on the icon bar.

2 Enter the check number, **1003**, date, **1/09/97**, and payee, **Apple Computer Inc**. Then press the **Tab** key.

3 The Open PO's Exist window appears because when you entered Apple Computer as the payee, QuickBooks searched its open purchase orders list to see if any already existed for this vendor. Click **Yes** to reveal the Open Purchase Orders window.

4 Click once near the **1/02/97** date in the Open Purchase Orders window to place a check on the PO No. 3001 line, then click **OK**.

5 The completed check appears with all the appropriate information to record the payment for the inventory. See Figure 3.8. Click **OK** to record the check.

Enter this information first

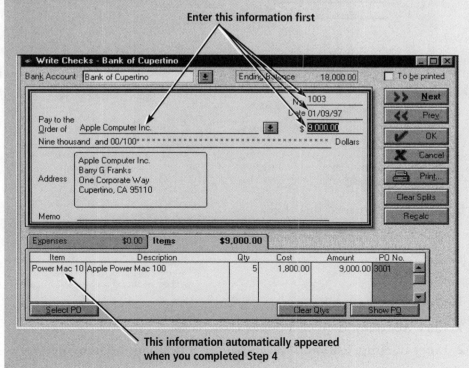

Figure 3.8
Completed Check Number 1003

This information automatically appeared when you completed Step 4

Liability insurance is a must for today's businesses, and Phoenix is no exception. Often premiums are paid in advance, and this is what Casey had to do at Phoenix—he wrote a check for an insurance prepayment. Karen watches as you demonstrate how QuickBooks records this type of transaction.

To write a check for liability insurance:

1 Click the **Check** button on the icon bar.

2 Enter the check number, **1001**, date, **1/07/97**, and payee, **Walker Insurance**, then press the **Tab** key. Note that since Walker Insurance is a new name, QuickBooks requires more information.

3 Click **Set up** in the Name Not Found window, click **Vendor**, and then click **OK**.

4 In the New Vendor window, create a new vendor: Walker Insurance, Ms. Pamela Walker, 10778 Edgewood Way, Cupertino, CA 95110. Click **OK** after you enter this information.

5 Enter **1,384.67** as the amount, and record this transaction by increasing a Prepaid Insurance account. This is a new account; set it up as an Other Current Asset Type as shown in Figure 3.9, and click **OK**.

Figure 3.9

Entering a New Account

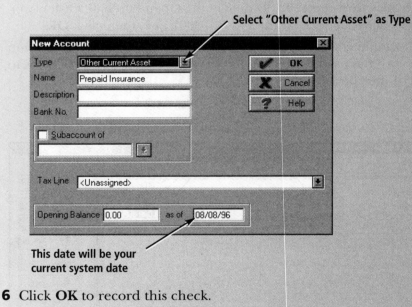

Select "Other Current Asset" as Type

This date will be your current system date

6 Click **OK** to record this check.

You now want to show Karen how QuickBooks accounts for two recent cash sales.

To record two cash sales:

1 Click **Activities**, then click **Enter Cash Sales**.

2 Enter the information shown in Figure 3.10 up to the Item box.

Click here to select customer   **Start with 501**

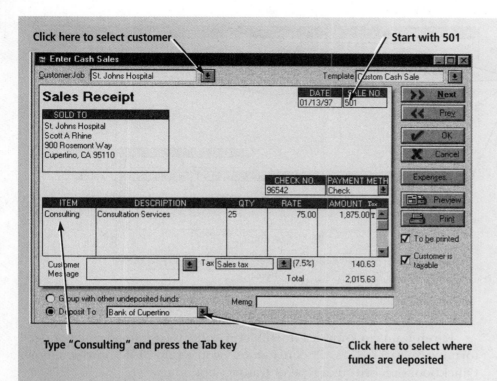

Type "Consulting" and press the Tab key   **Click here to select where funds are deposited**

Figure 3.10
Sales Receipt 501

3 Type **Consulting** in the Item column, then press the **Tab** key.

4 This is a new account, and therefore it requires set up. Enter the information specified in Figure 3.11 in the New Item window, including the account information, then click **OK**.

Click here to specify that this item is taxable

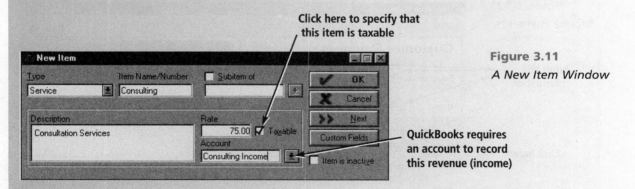

QuickBooks requires an account to record this revenue (income)

Figure 3.11
A New Item Window

5 Type **25** in the Qty column, then click the **Deposit To** button.

6 Click **Bank of Cupertino** as the bank into which funds are deposited. Be sure the box labeled "Customer is taxable" is checked.

7 Click **Next** to enter this sales receipt and prepare to record another. A new Enter Cash Sales window appears.

8 Enter the information shown in Figure 3.12.

9 Click **OK** to record this sales receipt.

Figure 3.12
Sales Receipt 502

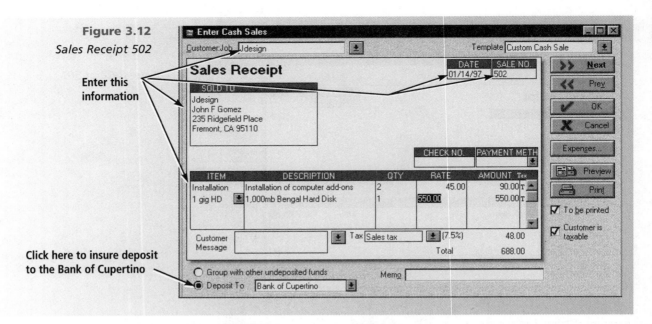

Karen wants to know if Phoenix ever collects cash in advance of performing services. "Yes, Phoenix does," you reply. "I'll show you how QuickBooks records that type of transaction."

To record receipt of advance payment:

1 Click **Activities**, then click **Receive Payments**.

2 Enter the information provided in Figure 3.13, then click **OK**.

Figure 3.13
Receive Payments Window

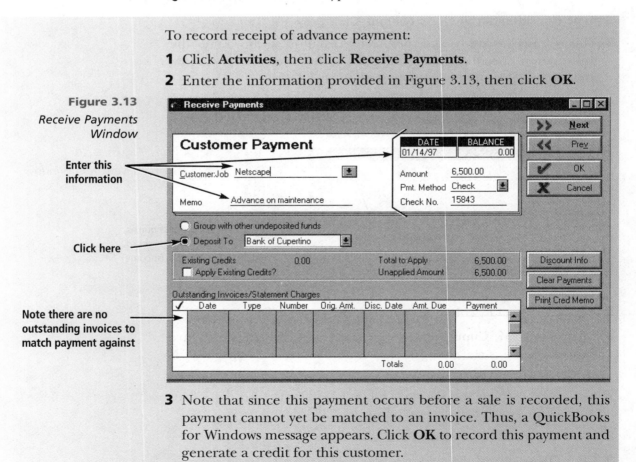

3 Note that since this payment occurs before a sale is recorded, this payment cannot yet be matched to an invoice. Thus, a QuickBooks for Windows message appears. Click **OK** to record this payment and generate a credit for this customer.

When Karen saw how Casey had recorded this transaction, she was perplexed. She knew that, strictly speaking, this transaction should have resulted in increases both to Cash and to a special liability account called "Advances to Customers," rather than in an increase to Cash and a decrease to Accounts Receivable. It became clear to her, however, that this approach would ultimately work when the sale was made and the invoice was generated.

Karen has one last question about QuickBooks transactions at Phoenix. "Does QuickBooks handle your payroll too?" she asks.

"Absolutely," you reply. "Let me show you our January payroll. Besides you, two of Phoenix's employees are on salary, and one employee is hourly."

To record and pay employees:

1 Click **Activities**, click **Payroll**, and then click **Pay Employees**.

2 Click **OK** in the Pay Employees window, since this is the first payroll for Phoenix.

3 Change the dates as shown in Figure 3.14. Click the **Mark All** button then click **Create**.

trouble? If the tax tables in your version of QuickBooks are for a prior period, a message box will appear warning you that the tax tables are not valid for this date. Click **OK** to ignore this message for now.

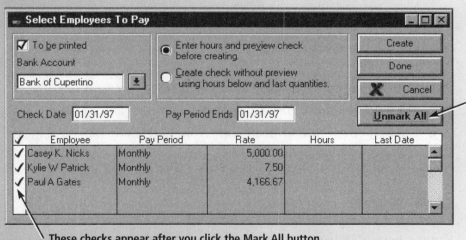

Figure 3.14
Select Employees to Pay

Click this button if you need to unmark employees for payment—this button toggles between Mark All and Unmark All

These checks appear after you click the Mark All button

4 Click **Create** to accept payroll information for Casey Nicks.

5 Type **160** in the Hours column as shown in Figure 3.15, then click **Create** to enter payroll information for Kylie Patrick.

trouble? The tax withholding and expenses shown here may be different from that shown on your screen. The data shown was created with tax table 9706. Check with your instructor to see which tax table your version of QuickBooks is using.

Figure 3.15

*Preview Paycheck Window
for Kylie Patrick*

Enter hours here

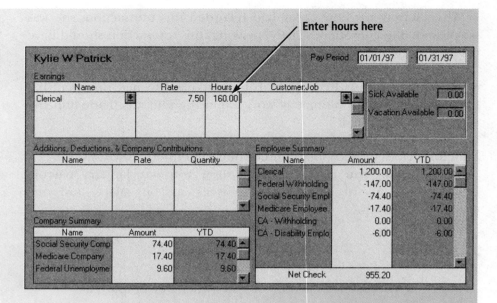

6 Click **Create** to accept payroll information for Paul A. Gates.

7 Click **Done** in the Select Employees To Pay window.

8 Close all open Windows and exit QuickBooks.

trouble? QuickBooks often prompts you to back up your data to avoid accidental data loss. If this message appears you may choose to accept or cancel this action. If you are storing your data on a floppy disk, *do not* use the QuickBooks backup feature unless you intend to back up to a disk drive other than the one on which your data is currently stored. Alternatively, quit QuickBooks and use either the Windows 3.1 File Manager to make a disk to disk copy. In Windows 95 you would:

a In My Computer, click the icon for the disk you want to copy.

b On the File menu, click **Copy Disk**.

c Click the drive you want to copy from and the drive you want to copy to, and then click **Start**.

END NOTE

. . . .

You've helped Karen understand some basic QuickBooks features including how to make deposits, write checks, create purchase orders, receive inventory, record cash sales, and create payroll.

Karen tells you that she is very impressed with QuickBooks's capabilities. Even after this brief overview of cash-oriented activities—whether they are financing, investing, or operating—she can see how QuickBooks will help her be a very effective and productive Phoenix employee.

practice

Chapter 3 Questions

1 Compare and contrast operating, investing, and financing activities.

2 Which menu in QuickBooks contains the option for making deposits?

3 How do you create a new account in QuickBooks, and what information is required?

4 How do you write checks in QuickBooks, and what information is required?

5 How do you create a purchase order in QuickBooks, and what information is required?

6 How do you record the receipt and payment of inventory in QuickBooks, and what information is required?

7 How do you record cash sales in QuickBooks, and what information is required?

8 How do you record the receipt of cash payments in QuickBooks, and what information is required?

9 How do you record payroll in QuickBooks, and what information is required?

10 Where does the payroll information used in recording payroll originate?

Chapter 3 Assignment

1 *Adding More Information to Phoenix Systems, Inc.*

For this Assignment use phnx03cp.qbw from your Student Disk. Add the following financing, investing, and operating activities, and then create and print a standard balance sheet as of March 31, 1997 and a standard income statement for the period January 1, 1997 to March 31, 1997.

Add the following financing activities:

a. Phoenix enters into a long-term loan agreement with New Endeavors for $25,000 on February 24, 1997. The loan is repayable at $500 per month. *Hint:* Use the Make Deposits activity to record this transaction. Enter "Long-Term Debt" in the From Account.

b. On March 11, 1997, Phoenix borrows $3,000 from the Bank of Cupertino on a short-term basis. *Hint:* Use the Make Deposits activity to record this transaction, use Quick Add to set up the Bank of Cupertino as an Other type, and create a new Short-term Debt account as an other current liability.

Add the following investing activities:

c. On January 17, 1997, Phoenix writes check 1006 to purchase furniture from Office Mart for $3,756.44. *Hint:* Create a new Furniture account as a fixed asset account and two subaccounts —cost and accumulated depreciation.

d. Phoenix makes an additional $10,000 investment with Sky Investments using check 1014 on February 4, 1997.

Add the following Phoenix operating activities:

e. Purchase Order 3008 is created on February 1, 1997, to Computer Wholesale for the purchase of ten 1 MB memory modules.

f. Purchase Order 3006 is created on February 5, 1997, to Bengal Drives for the purchase of five 800 MB hard drives and three 1 gigabyte hard drives.

g. Check 1015 is written on February 25, 1997, for $2,600 to Bengal Drives for receipt and payment of products requested on Purchase Order 3006.

h. Check 1002 is written to E-Max Realty on January 8, 1997, for $1,600 as payment of first and last months' rent. The check is properly recorded as Prepaid Rent, a current asset account. *Hint:* Set up E-Max Realty as a new vendor, contact Sonny Q. Bono, 93778 Texas Ave., Cupertino, CA 95110, 408-555-1130.

i. A $2,500 check (4930) is received from Boston Stores on March 6, 1997, and deposited as an advance on maintenance services. *Hint:* Set up Boston Stores as a new customer, contact Zack H. Haselmo, 10032 West 5th Street, Cupertino, CA 95110, 408-555-9874, terms net 15, customer is taxable. Record this payment, using QuickBooks's Receive Payments Activity and leave it as a credit for this customer, because no invoice has been created.

j. Payroll for the month ended February 28, 1997, is recorded and paid. Kylie Patrick worked 150 hours during this month.

k. A cash sale, SR 503, is recorded to Penny's Pet Parlor on February 7, 1997. The contact is Penny Purdue at 8499 Central Ave., Cupertino, CA 95110, 408-555-1975. The type is corporate and taxable (use the Additional Info tab in the New Customer window to set these parameters). The sale is for three hours of installation, a 1 gigabyte hard drive, and three 1 MB memory modules—all taxable. Penny pays with her check 1564 in the amount of $897.46. The check is held for deposit at a later time. *Hint:* Be sure to indicate on the sales receipt that this receipt is to be grouped with other undeposited funds.

l. A cash sale, SR 504, is recorded on February 21, 1997, to TRW. TRW's contact is Sally Q. Fairfield at 1000 Park Ave., Cupertino, CA 95110. The customer is taxable. The sale is for six 586-100 computers, 25 hours of consultation, and 5 hours of installation. TRW's check 504 is deposited directly into the Bank of Cupertino.

2 *Using the South-Western Home Page for More Assignments or Cases*

If you have Internet access, go to the home page for this textbook at owen.swcollege.com.

Select the **Chapter 3** section, and complete the problems(s) that your instructor assigns.

Chapter 3 Case Problem: JENNINGS & ASSOCIATES—Cash-Oriented Activities

In Chapter 2 you recreated Kelly Jennings' QuickBooks file as of January 1, 1997 because a virus had infected and corrupted her file. Later, an associate reentered all the transactions for January 1997. Now Kelly wants you to record the cash-oriented activities that occurred in February 1997.

Assignment:

Use the file named kj03cp.qbw from your Student Disk to record the following activities. Then, print a standard balance sheet as of February 28, 1997 and a standard income statement for the month of February 1997.

Financing Activities

1 On February 1, 1997, the company deposited cash contributions to First Valley Savings and Loan of $20,000 from Kelly Jennings (employee) and recorded them as capital stock.

2 On February 15, 1997, the company deposited cash contributions to First Valley Savings and Loan of $50,000 from a local investor (Frugal Investments) and recorded them as capital stock. (This is a new name and must be set up. Use the Quick Add feature.)

Investing Activities

3 On February 2, 1997, the company purchased $3,000 of computer equipment from Phoenix Computers issuing check number 1001 out of a First Valley Savings and Loan checking account.

4 On February 4, 1997, the company invested $5,000 with Dean Witter acquiring short-term investments (an other current asset) and paying with check number 1002 out of a First Valley Savings and Loan checking account. (Use the Quick Add and Set Up features of QuickBooks to add a new name and new account.)

Operating Activities

5   On February 7, 1997, the company ordered ten rolls of high quality film from Rex's Film Supply with Purchase Order number 4. Delivery is expected February 10, 1997.

6   On February 10, 1997, the company received the film ordered on Purchase Order number 4 and paid the bill with check number 1003 from a First Valley Savings and Loan checking account. *Hint:* Use the Write Checks Activity to record this transaction and receive inventory on Purchase Order number 4.

7   On February 12, 1997, the company issued check number 1004 for $75 to Bruno's Stationers to pay for office supplies purchased during the month. (Use Quick Add for this vendor.)

8   On February 10, 1997, the company completed a cash sale to Yaskar Farms (Sale No. 50001), for 35 hours of promotional campaign work, 5 rolls of high quality film, and 2 rolls of regular film. Yaskar wrote their check number 5677 to pay for this sale. The payment was deposited directly to the Union Bank checking account.

9   On February 22, 1997, the company completed a cash sale to AAA Appliance Co. (Sale No. 50002), who paid for this sale with their check number 1344. AAA was invoiced for 75 hours for a magazine layout and 40 rolls of regular film. The payment was deposited directly to the Union Bank checking account.

10   On February 26, 1997, the company received a $2,000 check (2999) from Bob and Mary Schultz as an advance payment for services to be rendered next month. The amount is recorded as a credit to their receivable account. Deposit this check in the Union Bank checking account.

11   On February 15, 1997, and February 28, 1997, the company paid its employees. Kelly Jennings collected her salary based on an annual salary of $48,000. Diane worked 80 hours and 76 hours for the two pay periods, while Cheryl worked 79 and 73 hours for the two pay periods. Payroll checks are paid from the Union Bank checking account.

chapter
4

Additional Business Activities

In this chapter you will:

- Record transactions classified as financing activities, such as borrowing from banks and repaying previous loans

- Record transactions classified as investing activities, such as selling short-term investments

- Record transactions classified as operating activities, such as purchasing inventory on account and selling that inventory on account

- Recording transactions classified as non-cash investing and financing activities, such as purchasing equipment with long-term debt

CASE: PHOENIX SYSTEMS CONSULTING, INC.

At your next meeting with Karen, you explain to her that Phoenix Systems engaged in financing, investing, and operating activities during the first three months of 1997 in addition to those already discussed (in Chapter 3). Karen suggests that you look at these additional transactions in the same order as before—financing, investing, and operating.

RECORDING ADDITIONAL FINANCING ACTIVITIES

You tell Karen that Phoenix often engages in financing activities such as borrowing funds and paying back previous loans. You suggest looking at some loan activity that took place during the quarter. For example, in January Phoenix borrowed $12,500 from the Bank of Cupertino. Then in March Phoenix repaid $10,500 of this loan by writing a check.

To record the deposit:

1 Open phnx04.qbw located on your Student Disk.

2 Click **Activities** and then click **Make Deposits**.

3 Before the Make Deposits window appears, a Payments to Deposit window is shown. QuickBooks will prompt you to choose a payment if any payment had been recorded but not yet deposited. The payment shown in this window will be deposited later. For now click **Cancel**.

4 Select **Bank of Cupertino** in the Deposit To edit box.

5 Enter the Date, Received From, Amount, and From Account information as shown in Figure 4.1 to record the deposit.

Figure 4.1
The Make Deposits Window

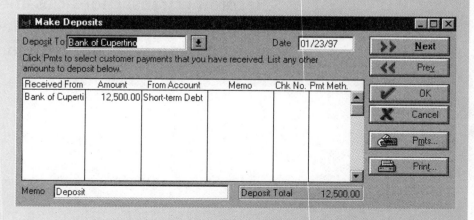

6 Click **OK** to record the deposit.

A couple of months later, Phoenix repaid part of the loan. You show Karen how to record the repayment.

To record repayment:

1 Click the **Check** button on the icon bar.

2 Enter the check number, **1024**, date, **3/24/97**, payee, **Bank of Cupertino**, amount, **10,500**, and account, **Short-term debt**, as shown in Figure 4.2

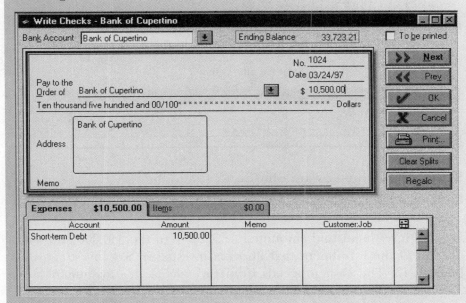

Figure 4.2

The Write Checks Window

3 Click **OK** to record the check.

Karen asks how you'd record a loan in QuickBooks if you purchase new equipment by borrowing funds—in other words a non-cash financing and investing activity.

"We'll get to that in a minute," you reply. " First let's cover some additional cash-oriented activities."

RECORDING ADDITIONAL INVESTING ACTIVITIES

You know from your accounting course that investing activities generally result in the acquisition of non-current assets from buying or selling investment securities or productive equipment. During the first quarter of 1997, Phoenix Systems engaged in two particular investing activities that you want to show Karen—the company transferred additional funds from the Bank of Cupertino to its short-term investments account, and it sold previously purchased investment securities for a profit.

Recall from Chapter 3 that Phoenix transferred $8,000 from its checking account to its Short-term Investments account on January 10. On February 24, Phoenix transfers $7,000 more to this account.

To record this additional transfer:

1 Click the **Accnt** button on the icon bar.

2 Click **Short-term Investments** in the Chart of Accounts window then click **Activities**, then click **Use Register** to reveal the Short-term Investments register.

3 Click in the **1-Line** check box—found in the lower-middle portion of the Register window—to change the look of the register to that shown in Figure 4.3 below.

4 Enter the date, the account, and the deposit information as shown in Figure 4.3. Then click **Record** to record the $7,000 deposit.

Figure 4.3
The Short-Term Investment Register

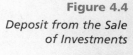

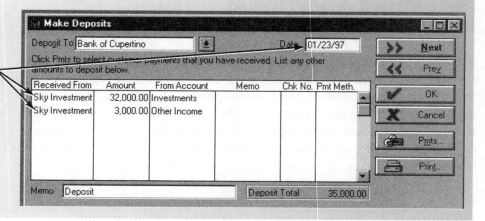

5 Close the Short-term Investments Register window.

6 Close the Chart of Accounts window.

The investment sold amounted to $32,000 of the $40,000 and was a portion of the investment that Phoenix invested in Sky Investments on January 13. The cash proceeds from the sale of this investment were $35,000, which, as you will see, means that Phoenix earned a $3,000 profit.

To record the sale of an investment and the resulting deposit of funds:

1 Click **Activities** and then **Make Deposits**.

2 Before the Make Deposits window appears, a Payments to Deposit window is shown. For now click **Cancel**.

3 Select **Bank of Cupertino** in the Deposit To edit box. Then enter the date and then the receipt of $35,000—$32,000 from the original investment and a profit of $3,000—as shown in Figure 4.4.

Figure 4.4
Deposit from the Sale of Investments

4 Click **OK** to record this deposit.

RECORDING ADDITIONAL OPERATING ACTIVITIES

Now that you've seen how QuickBooks handles additional financing and investing activities, you want to show Karen how QuickBooks records invoices when sales are recorded before the receipt of cash; in other words—sales on account. You'll also show her inventory purchases on account.

As you've seen earlier, Phoenix uses purchase orders to help manage its inventory. These are used even if purchases are made on account.

To create a purchase order for merchandise purchased on account:

1 Click the **PO** button on the icon bar.

2 Enter the Vendor, Date, P.O. Number, Item, and Quantity information as shown in Figure 4.5. QuickBooks will automatically fill in the Description, Rate, and Amount.

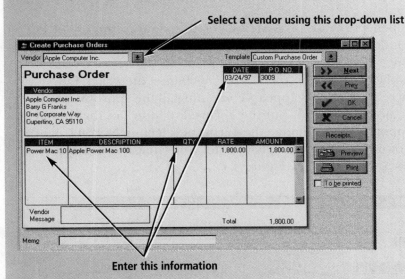

Select a vendor using this drop-down list

Enter this information

Figure 4.5

Purchase Order 3009

3 Click **OK** to record the purchase.

You must also use a purchase order when inventory is received along with a bill requesting payment.

To record the receipt of inventory ordered and the related bill:

1 Click **Activities**, click **Inventory**, and then click **Receive Items and Enter Bill** as shown in Figure 4.6.

Figure 4.6

*The Menu Selection
to Receive Inventory
and Enter a Bill*

**Click and hold the
mouse here to view the
sub-menu shown**

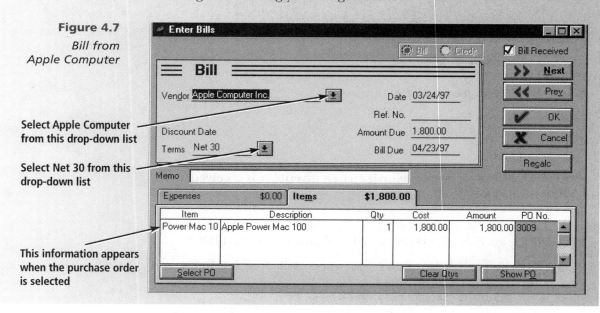

2 Select **Apple Computer** from the drop-down Vendor list in the Enter
Bills window.

3 Since open purchase orders exist for this vendor, the Open PO's
Exist window appears. Click **Yes**.

4 Click once near the **3/24/97** date in the Open Purchase Orders window to place a check on the PO No. 3009 line, then click **OK**.

5 The corresponding bill appears containing all the appropriate information already filled in. But the Terms line indicates that payment
is due upon receipt. Change the Terms by selecting **Net 30** from the
drop-down Terms list and, as you do, note that the Bill Due date
changes accordingly. See Figure 4.7.

Figure 4.7

*Bill from
Apple Computer*

**Select Apple Computer
from this drop-down list**

**Select Net 30 from this
drop-down list**

**This information appears
when the purchase order
is selected**

6 Click **OK** to record the receipt of inventory and enter the bill.

7 Since you changed the terms for Apple Computer, QuickBooks displays a Name Information Changed window. Click **NO** to maintain the old terms.

"Cash sales are the best!" Casey exclaims as he enters the room.

"Not necessarily," Karen responds. "Phoenix might be losing quality customers if you're not offering credit terms."

"Of course, you're right," Casey quickly agrees. "I was just kidding. We often sell on credit to customers who've demonstrated credit worthiness. As long as we keep good records and monitor tardy customers, we don't take too much of a risk extending credit. Show her some of our credit sales," Casey suggests.

To record credit sales:

1 Click the **Invoice button** on the icon bar.

2 Change the custom template from Intuit Service Invoice to Intuit Professional Invoice.

3 Enter the Customer, Date, Invoice Number, the two Items sold, and their respective Quantities as shown in Figure 4.8. QuickBooks will automatically enter the other information and calculate the total.

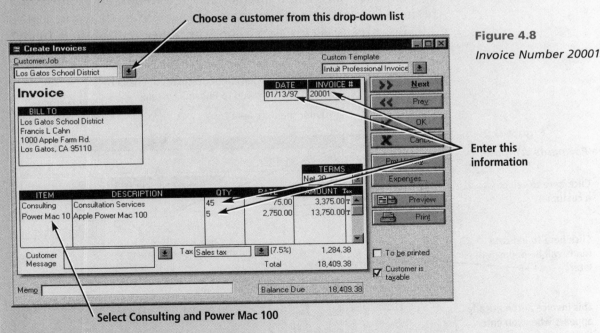

Figure 4.8

Invoice Number 20001

4 Click **Next**.

5 The credit limit for Los Gatos is $10,000, and this invoice exceeds that amount. Since this is just a practice session for Karen, you decide to click **Yes** to allow the sale.

6 You decide to give Karen more practice. Enter the following two invoices:

Customer	Date	Invoice #	Terms	Item	Quantity
St. Johns	1/20/97	20002	Net 15	Maintenance	100
Netscape	3/31/97	20007	2% 10 Net 30	Maintenance	60

7 Click **OK** to enter the last invoice and close the Create Invoices window.

"I'm not an accountant," Casey says, "but don't you have to wait until the customer pays before recording this sale?"

"No," replies Karen, "because on the accrual basis—which Phoenix uses—revenue is recognized when Phoenix delivers the product or performs the service."

"What happens when the customer pays us?" asks Casey.

"Then we use the Receive Payments activity," you explain. "I'll show you."

To record receipt of payment from previously recorded sales:

1 Click **Activities**, then click **Receive Payments**.

2 On February 14, 1997, Phoenix received payments from two customers. The first was from the Los Gatos School District for $18,409.38 to pay Invoice number 20001. Carefully enter the appropriate information for this customer payment as shown in Figure 4.9. Be sure to click the **"Group with other undeposited funds"** option button. Then click **Next** to record this receipt.

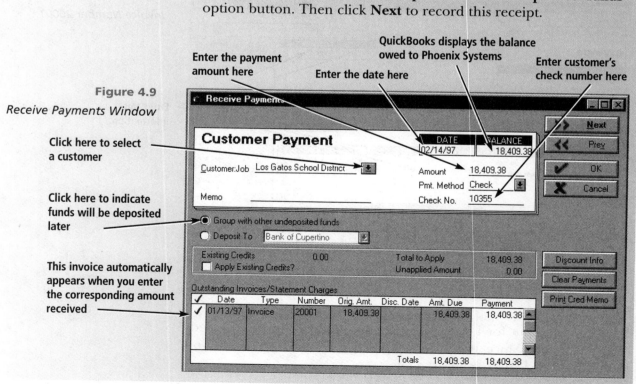

Figure 4.9

Receive Payments Window

3 The second payment received was $5,375 from St. Johns Hospital for Invoice Number 20002 with their check 89544. This payment was also grouped with other undeposited funds. Carefully enter the appropriate information in the Receive Payments window. Then click **OK**.

"When are these funds deposited?" asks Karen.

"In this case a deposit was made on February 16, 1997," you reply. "Casey deposited all receipts received that week. Let me show you how QuickBooks handles deposits of previously recorded receipts." .

To record the deposit of previously recorded receipts:

1 Click **Activities**, then click **Make Deposits**. The Payments to Deposit Window appears. See Figure 4.10.

When all payments are selected, check marks appear here

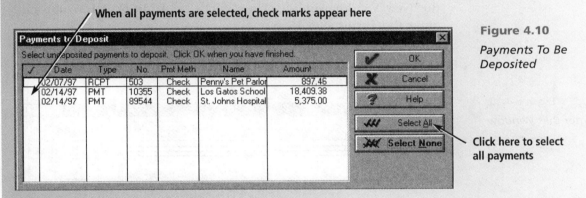

Figure 4.10

Payments To Be Deposited

Click here to select all payments

2 Three receipts are shown in the Payments to Deposit window. Click **Select All** to select all receipts for deposit, then click **OK**. The Make Deposits window appears. See Figure 4.11.

Change the date here

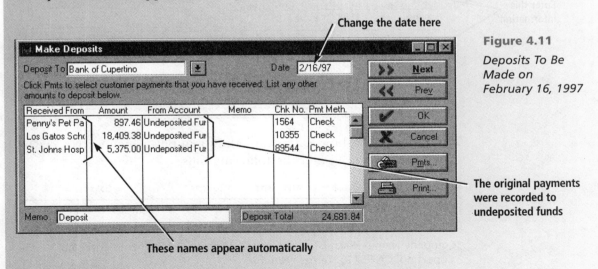

Figure 4.11

Deposits To Be Made on February 16, 1997

The original payments were recorded to undeposited funds

These names appear automatically

3 Change the date in the Make Deposits window to **02/16/97**, then click **OK** to record the deposit.

"Does Phoenix always immediately pay cash for expenses?" asks Karen.

"No, not since we've been able to establish credit with our vendors and they've extended us terms," you answer. "We record our bills during the month as they come in, and then we pay them at the end of each month. Let me show you how we recorded some bills in January."

To record some January bills:

1 Click **Activities**, then click **Enter Bills**. The Enter Bills window appears.

2 Enter **GTE** in the Vendor section of the Enter Bills window, then press the **Tab** key.

3 Since GTE is a new vendor, the Vendor Not Found window appears. Click **Set Up**.

4 Enter the Company Name, **GTE**, and the address, **3899 Stevens Creek #230, Cupertino, CA 95110** in the Address Info tab section of the New Vendor window. Then click the **Additional Info** tab and enter the Terms, **Net 15**.

5 Click **OK** to enter this new vendor information.

6 Enter the additional GTE bill information as shown in Figure 4.12, then click **Next**.

Figure 4.12

Enter Bills Window

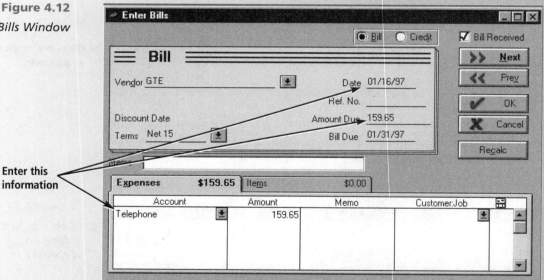

Enter this information

7 You decide to show Karen two additional bills which were received on the same day. Enter the following bills.

Vendor	Date	Amount	Terms	Expense
PG&E *	1/16/97	$230.00	Net 15	Utilities: Gas and Electric
Office Mart	1/16/97	$560.00	Net 15	Office Supplies

*Company Name—Pacific Gas & Electric, Address—9100 Town Center Dr., Cupertino, CA 95110, Terms—Net 15

8 Click **OK** after you enter both bills. (Click **No** in the "You have changed some information" window that appears.)

You then explain to Karen that, at the end of the month, all of these bills were paid. To pay bills using QuickBooks you use the Pay Bills activity.

To pay the January bills and print checks:

1 Click **Activities**, then click **Pay Bills**.

2 Enter the Payment Date, **1/29/97** and change the Show bills due on or before date to **1/31/97**.

3 In the Pay By box, choose "Check" and "To be printed" and make sure the correct bank account is showing. See Figure 4.13. Then press the **Tab** key.

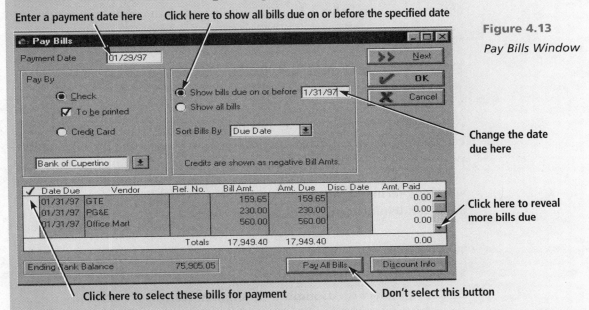

Figure 4.13

Pay Bills Window

4 Select the **GTE**, **PG&E**, and **Office Mart** bills to pay by clicking once next to each vendor's date due in the Check column. Then click **OK**.

trouble? Do not select the Pay All Bills button. Below the three most current bills shown is another bill from Computer Wholesale that will be paid later.

5 Click **File**, click **Print Forms**, click **Print Checks**.

6 Click on "Print company name and address" in the Print Checks window. Note that all the checks that appear are selected for payment.

7 Change the First Check Number to **1007** as shown in Figure 4.14, then click **OK**.

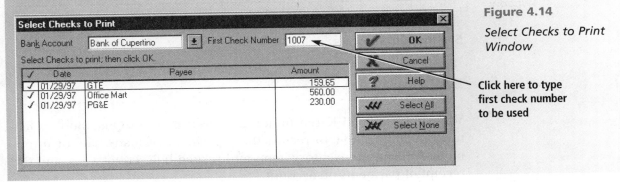

Figure 4.14

Select Checks to Print Window

8 Be sure your printer is turned on and ready to print. Click **OK** in the Print Checks window then click **Print** in the Print Checks window. After the checks have printed, click **OK** in the Did check(s) print OK? window.

You've now explained and demonstrated to Karen the financing, investing, and operating activities that are typical at Phoenix Systems. But there remains one transaction that you haven't yet shown her—one that is classified as a non-cash investing and financing activity. This transaction, you both believe, is just as important as the cash transactions.

RECORDING NON-CASH INVESTING AND FINANCING ACTIVITIES

Although non-cash investing and financing activities do not affect the cash position of a company, they do have an impact on a firm's financial position. One example of such an activity was Phoenix's purchase of computer equipment in March of 1997 that was completely financed with long-term debt. You explain the nature of this transaction to Karen and now demonstrate how it was recorded.

To record the purchase of equipment with long-term debt:

1 Click **Accnt** on the icon bar.
2 Click to select the **Computer Equipment:Cost** account in the Chart of Accounts window, then click **Activities**, then click **Use Register**.
3 Click in the **1-Line** check box to make columns easier to input information.
4 Fill in the information for the second entry in this register as shown in Figure 4.15: the Date, **03/31/97**, the Payee, **IBM**, the Account, **Long-Term Debt**, and the Increase, **$15,000**. Then click **Record** to record the transaction.

Figure 4.15

The Computer Equipment: Cost Register Window

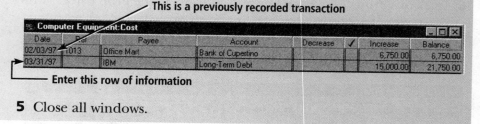

5 Close all windows.

END NOTE

You've now helped Karen understand even more of QuickBooks's features including how to record the repayment of loans, sale of investments, receipt of inventory items and related bills, credit sales, and the receipt of payments on account.

practice

Chapter 4 Questions

1 Describe two ways you can create purchase orders in QuickBooks.

2 How do you record the receipt of inventory and bills in QuickBooks, and what information is required?

3 How do you access vendor names from the Enter Bills window?

4 What payment terms are available in QuickBooks when entering bills?

5 Consider this statement: "QuickBooks records revenue when an invoice is generated even though cash has not been received." Is this practice acceptable? Why or why not?

6 Identify the QuickBooks activity required to record payments received on account.

7 Should payments received on account be deposited immediately? If yes, why? If no, what account is increased to record these receipts?

8 How does the QuickBooks software respond if a bill is entered with a vendor name not included on the vendor list?

9 What are non-cash investing and financing activities, and how are they recorded in QuickBooks?

10 Describe the QuickBooks process for printing checks.

Chapter 4 Assignments

1 ***Adding More Information to Phoenix Systems, Inc.***

For this assignment use phnx04cp.qbw from your Student Disk. Add the following financing, investing, and operating activities. Then create a standard balance sheet as of March 31, 1997 and a standard income statement for the period January 1, 1997 through March 31, 1997.

Add the following financing activities:

a. On March 31, 1997, Phoenix borrows $40,000 from the Bank of Sedona (because this is a new name, use Quick Add and add as name type: Other). The loan is due September 30, 1998, with interest at 10%. These funds are deposited into the Bank of Cupertino account.

b. On March 28, 1997, Phoenix pays New Endeavors $500 as partial repayment of debt (no interest) with check 1031.

Add the following investing activities:

c. On February 25, 1997, Phoenix sells $6,000 of their investment with Sky Investments for $5,000, thereby incurring a $1,000 investment loss. (Record as a reduction in Other Income similar to the text example where income was earned. In this case, however, the loss is entered as a negative number.

An equivalent approach is to record the loss as an increase in Other Expense.)

d. On January 17, 1997, Phoenix transfers $2,000 from the Short-term Investments account to the Bank of Cupertino checking account.

Add the following operating activities:

e. On January 24, 1997, Phoenix generates Purchase Order 3005 to IBM to purchase three IBM Pentium computers at a cost of $7,500 each. (*Note*: This item has already been set up in your QuickBooks data file.)

f. On February 6, 1997, the computers ordered under PO 3005 are received and a bill is recorded.

g. Phoenix creates the following invoices. Notice how Quick-Books warns you that the Los Gatos School District has exceeded its credit limit. When this warning appears, click **Yes.** (If terms change for any customer, accept the change as permanent.)

Date	Invoice #	Customer	Customer PO #	Terms	Product	Qty
2/19/97	20003	Netscape	542215	2% 10 Net 30	586-160 Consultation Installation	5 4 10
3/26/97	20006	Los Gatos School District	none	Net 30	IBM Pentium Consultation	3 5
3/31/97	20008	Boston Stores	none	Net 15	Monthly Maintenance	30

h. On February 18, 1997, Phoenix receives the following bills: (If terms change for any vendor, accept the change as permanent.)

Vendor	Operating Expense	Terms	Amount
E-Max Realty	Rent	Net 15	800.00
GTE	Telephone	Net 15	92.56
Office Mart	Office supplies	Net 15	32.56
PG&E	Utilities: Gas and Electric	Net 15	179.00

i. On February 27, 1997, Phoenix pays the following bills: (*Hint:* Use a two-step process; that is, pay the bills first, then print checks. Also be sure to click the **Show All Bills** box in the Pay Bills window.)

Vendor	Check #	Amount
Computer Wholesale	1016	15,199.75
E-Max Realty	1017	800.00
GTE	1018	92.56
Office Mart	1019	32.56
PG&E	1020	179.00

j. Phoenix receives payments (checks) from customers as follows: (*Note*: Deposits for each payment were made to the Bank of Cupertino on the day following the payment date.)

Date	Customer	Apply to Invoice #	Amount
3/19/97	Netscape	20003	10,250.00
3/19/97	St. Johns Hospital	20005	500.00
3/27/97	Los Gatos School Dist.	20006	5,000.00

k. Phoenix has one non-cash investing and financing activity on March 31, 1997 in which computer equipment is acquired from Apple Computer Inc. in exchange for a long-term note payable of $7,000 due in two years.

2   *Using the South-Western Home Page for More Assignments or Cases*

If you have Internet access, go to the home page for this textbook at owen.swcollege.com.

Select the **Chapter 4** section and complete the problem(s) that your instructor assigns.

Go to
owen.swcollege.com

http://

Chapter 4 Case Problem: JENNINGS & ASSOCIATES—Cash-Oriented Activities

In Chapter 2 you recreated Kelly Jennings' QuickBooks file as of January 1, 1997, because a virus had infected and corrupted her file. Later, an associate reentered all the transactions for January 1997. You entered the transactions that took place in February 1997, in Chapter 3. Now Kelly wants you to enter additional transactions that occurred in March 1997.

Assignment:

Use the file named kj04cp.qbw from your Student Disk to record the following transactions. (*Note:* Additional transactions have already been entered into this file for you that were not included in Chapter 3, so do not use your completed kj03cp.qbw file.) After entering the transactions, print a standard balance sheet as of 3/31/97 and a standard income statement (profit & loss) for the month ended 3/31/97.

Financing Activities

1   On March 1, 1997, the company deposits $8,000 into the First Valley Savings & Loan account as the proceeds from a short-term note payable agreement between First Valley Savings & Loan and Jennings & Associates.

2   On March 2, 1997, the company issues check 1005 from First Valley Savings & Loan to pay off a $5,000 loan from the Bank of San Martin.

Investing Activities

3 On March 3, 1997 the company sells some short-term investments, which had cost $3,000, for a $500 profit. The proceeds of the sale from Dean Witter were deposited immediately to First Valley Savings & Loan.

4 On March 4, 1997 the company purchases computer equipment from Phoenix Computers for $7,000 using check 1006 written from the First Valley Savings & Loan account.

Operating Activities

5 On March 6, 1997 the company orders 50 rolls of regular film from Rex's Film Supply that were expected by March 10, 1997. Use Purchase Order number 5.

6 On March 10 the company receives the film ordered under Purchase Order number 5 and records a bill.

7 The company records the following invoices: (Accept all changes in terms as permanent.)

Date	Invoice #	Customer	Customer PO #	Terms	Product	Qty
3/15/97	13	Bob and Mary Schultz	5611	Net 30	Magazine Layout	5
					HQ Film	3
3/18/97	14	Yaskar Farms	B23	Net 30	Press Release	5
3/25/97	15	Fancy Yogurt	9988	Net 15	TV Commercial	75

8 The company receives the following bills on March 18, 1997: (Accept all changes in terms as permanent.)

Vendor	Operating Expense	Terms	Amount
Frank Mendez Properties	Rent	Net 15	700.00
Pacific Electric	Utilities: Gas and Electric	Net 15	65.00
KCOY TV	TV Commercial Spots	Net 15	7,500.00
Owen & Owen	Professional Fees: Legal Fees	Net 15	375.00

9 On March 29, 1997, the company pays all bills due as of March 31. Bills are paid out of the First Valley Savings & Loan account starting with check number 1007. Do not print checks. *(Hint:* Total payments should total $7,156.50. Remember, pay only bills due as of 3/31/97. If your total payments are different, check to make sure you entered the correct dates and payment terms for all bills.)

10 The company receives the following payments (checks) from customers: (*Note*: Deposits for each payment were made to the First Valley Savings & Loan on the same day.)

Date	Customer	Apply to Invoice #	Amount
3/26/97	Big 10	5	325.00
3/28/97	Evelyn Walker Real Estate	4	200.00
3/29/97	Ray's Chevron	8	650.00

Non-Cash Investing and Financing Activities

11 On March 15 the company purchased a small sport utility vehicle for $18,500. The purchase was 100% financed with a loan from First Valley Savings & Loan and bears monthly payments that will pay off the loan with interest at 10% in five years. (*Hint:* Create a Vehicles Fixed Asset account and two subaccounts—Cost and Accumulated Depreciation. Also create a Vehicle Loan: long-term liability account.)

chapter

5

Adjusting Entries

In this chapter you will:

- Accrue expenses incurred but not yet recorded
- Accrue revenue earned but not yet recorded
- Record the expiration of assets and their related expenses
- Record the reduction of unearned revenues and their related revenues
- Prepare a bank reconciliation and record related adjustments

CASE: PHOENIX SYSTEMS CONSULTING, INC.
· ·

Casey has recorded the majority of Phoenix's financing, investing, and operating activities for January through March 1997. To help him prepare financial statements for the first quarter, he asks Karen and you to prepare any necessary adjusting entries for the period January 1 through March 31, 1997.

"Some people have trouble with adjusting entries" Karen remarks, "but I'm not one of them. I was always helping my classmates understand these types of journal entries. Why don't I give them a try?"

"Okay with me," you respond. "Traditional journal entries are available in QuickBooks, but you don't have to use them." You explain that in QuickBooks the most common adjusting entries—accruing expenses, accruing revenue, recording asset expirations, and recording liability reductions—can be made by using the Enter Special Transactions menu item in the Activity menu or by using account registers. You decide to show the register method to Karen now, and use the journal entry process later.

ACCRUING EXPENSES
· ·

Phoenix borrowed $12,500 on a short-term basis from the Bank of Cupertino on January 23 and another $3,000 on March 11. On March 24, Phoenix repaid $10,500 of that $15,500 balance. The $5,000 ending balance on March 31 represents the principal owed on that date but does not include interest on the loan. The bank has just informed Phoenix that $250 of interest was charged to their loan balance due.

To accrue interest expense using QuickBooks's registers:

1 Open QuickBooks if it is not already open, then open phnx05.qbw from your Student Disk.

2 Click **Accnt** on the icon bar to display the chart of accounts.

3 Scroll down the chart of accounts and click **Short-term Debt**; then click the **Activities** button, then click **Use Register**.

4 Enter the date, **March 31, 1997**, the payee, **Bank of Cupertino**, and the increase, **250**, on the first line. Then select the account **Interest Expense:Loan Interest**.

5 Click **Record** to enter this transaction. The resulting adjustment is now reflected in the register as shown in Figure 5.1.

6 Close the Short-term Debt Register window. Keep the Chart of Accounts window open.

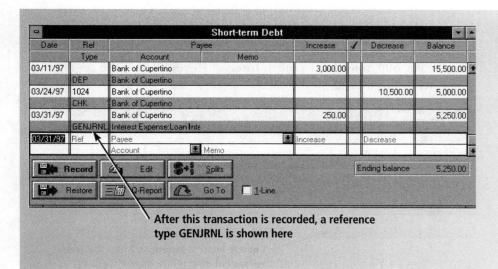

Figure 5.1
The Short-Term Debt Register

After this transaction is recorded, a reference
type GENJRNL is shown here

Most financial accounting textbooks illustrate the accrual of interest expenses by using an Interest Payable account, rather than a Short-term Debt account. Although either approach is acceptable, using a Short-term Debt account allows you to more quickly reconcile your records with the Bank of Cupertino's loan statement, which shows a $5,250 balance, as shown in Figure 5.1.

ACCRUING REVENUE

You tell Karen that she can also use registers to record revenue earned on investments. She recalls that during the quarter the company had some bond investments with Sky Investments that earned interest. The interest is paid semi-annually. Since no interest was paid during the quarter, no interest revenue has been recorded. After checking with their investment advisor, Karen learns that $500 interest revenue was earned but unpaid as of March 31, 1997. QuickBooks has a pre-established account for interest revenue although it is labeled interest income. Karen decides to change the account title first before accruing the interest.

To edit the Interest Income account and accrue interest revenue on an investment using a register:

1 Click the **Acct** button on the icon bar if the chart of accounts is not already open.

2 Click the **Interest Income** account located near the bottom of the Chart of Accounts. Click the **Account** button, then click **Edit** to edit the Interest Income account and change its name and description to **Interest Revenue**, then click **OK** in the Edit Account window.

3 Now select **Investments** from the Chart of Accounts window.

4 Click the **Activities** button, then click **Use Register**.

5 Type the date, **March 31, 1997**, the payee, **Sky Investments**, the increase, **500**, and the account, **Interest Revenue** into the register as shown in Figure 5.2.

Figure 5.2

The Investments Register

Date	Ref	Payee		Decrease	✓	Increase	Balance
	Type	Account	Memo				
01/23/97		Sky Investments		32,000.00			8,000.00
	DEP	Bank of Cupertino [split]					
02/04/97	1014	Sky Investments				10,000.00	18,000.00
	CHK	Bank of Cupertino					
02/25/97		Sky Investments		6,000.00			12,000.00
	DEP	Bank of Cupertino [split]					
03/31/97		Sky Investments				500.00	12,500.00
	DEP	Interest Revenue					

Change Interest Income to Interest Revenue before entering this account

6 Click **Record** to enter the adjustment.

7 Close the Investments Register window.

Although either approach is acceptable, some accountants prefer to separate the principal of the loan from the interest on the loan by using an Interest Receivable account rather than an Investments Other Current Asset account.

RECORDING THE EXPIRATION OF ASSETS AND THEIR RELATED EXPENSES

The two adjustments you've shown Karen accounted for previously unrecorded transactions. Next you want to show her how to record adjustments that affect previously recorded business activity, such as the prepayment of costs, the purchase of fixed assets, and the receipt of unearned revenue.

On January 7, 1997, Phoenix paid a premium of $1,384.67 to Walker Insurance for a one year liability insurance policy. Since this payment represented an expenditure that benefited more than the accounting period January 1 to March 31, it was correctly recorded to Prepaid Insurance, an asset account.

On March 31, 1997, one-fourth of the time period covered by the insurance had expired. Thus one-fourth of the cost ($346.17) should be recorded as liability insurance expense, and the prepaid insurance account reduced accordingly.

To adjust prepaid insurance using a register:

1 Click **Prepaid Insurance** from the Chart of Accounts window.

2 Click the **Activities** button, then click **Use Register**.

3 Type the date, **March 31, 1997**, the payee, **Walker Insurance**, and **346.17** in the Decrease column of line one. Then click the account, **Insurance:Liability Insurance**.

trouble? QuickBooks has preset expense accounts, some of which specify the term expense and some, like Insurance:Liability Insurance above, which do not. To be consistent, all expenses should include the expense term, but due to space limitations in report descriptions leave this one as is.

4 Click **Record** to enter the adjustment. The resulting adjustment is now recorded as shown in Figure 5.3.

Date	Ref	Payee		Decrease	✓	Increase	Balance
	Type	Account	Memo				
01/07/97	1001	Walker Insurance				1,384.67	1,384.67
	CHK	Bank of Cupertino					
03/31/97		Walker Insurance		346.17			1,038.50
	GENJRNL	Insurance:Liability Insurance					

(Prepaid Insurance register window)

Note the GENJRNL reference type

Figure 5.3
The Prepaid Insurance Register

5 Close the Prepaid Insurance Register window.

A similar adjustment called **depreciation** is needed to document the use or expiration of a previously recorded depreciable asset. Phoenix had purchased some computer equipment early in 1997 and had calculated depreciation expense of $375 for the period ending March 31, 1997. Depreciation on fixed assets is usually accumulated in a separate contra-asset account on the balance sheet for control purposes.

To record depreciation on the computer equipment:

1 Click **Accumulated Depreciation** located under the Computer Equipment account in the Chart of Accounts window, as shown in Figure 5.4, then click the **Activities** button, then click **Use Register**.

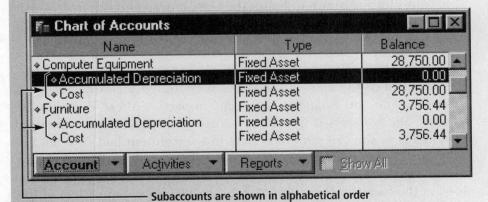

Subaccounts are shown in alphabetical order

Figure 5.4
Fixed Asset Accounts in the Chart of Accounts

2 Type the date, **March 31, 1997**, the decrease, **375.00**, and the account, **Depreciation Expense,** into the register. Note that the asset subaccount, Accumulated Depreciation, is decreased so as to reduce the asset itself. This will be less confusing if you, like the QuickBooks software, think of Accumulated Depreciation as an asset account that must be decreased to increase its normal negative balance. Meanwhile, the Depreciation Expense account has been increased.

3 Click **Record** to enter the adjustment.

4 Close the Accumulated Depreciation Register window.

Karen asks about the order of subaccounts shown in the Chart of Accounts window. In particular, she wonders why Accumulated Depreciation is listed before the asset's cost. You explain that QuickBooks automatically lists subaccounts in alphabetical order as shown in Figure 5.4. Karen is correct in questioning this order as standard presentation for these assets should reflect cost before accumulated depreciation. Before moving on you suggest a change in the order of these accounts using the Chart of Accounts.

To change the order of fixed asset subaccounts:

1 Scroll down the Chart of Accounts window to the fixed asset section.

2 Click and hold the cursor over the far left side of the Computer Equipment Accumulated Depreciation account. Note that the cursor changes to a four-arrow shape.

3 Drag the Accumulated Depreciation account to a place between Cost and the next account, then release the mouse button. (The Accumulated Depreciation account should now be shown below Cost.)

4 Repeat Steps 2 and 3 to move the Accumulated Depreciation account for Furniture to below the Cost subaccount.

5 Close the Chart of Accounts window.

Karen finds the above procedures very straightforward, but she is curious about the financial statement impact of these depreciation entries. She wonders if QuickBooks provides a way to view financial statements so she can see what effect this adjustment had. You tell her that QuickBooks does have such a feature—you can view financial statements at any time without having to post entries. You suggest that she look at the balance sheet as of March 31, 1997, to see the effect of this adjustment on the fixed assets.

To view the fixed assets portion of the balance sheet as of March 31, 1997:

1 Click **Reports** and then click **Balance Sheet:Standard**.

2 Enter the dates From 1/01/97 to 3/31/97 in the Customize Report window, then click **OK**.

3 Scroll down the balance sheet to the fixed assets section as shown in Figure 5.5.

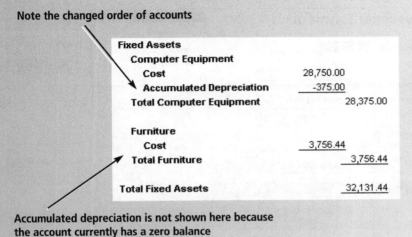

Note the changed order of accounts

Fixed Assets		
Computer Equipment		
Cost	28,750.00	
Accumulated Depreciation	-375.00	
Total Computer Equipment		28,375.00
Furniture		
Cost	3,756.44	
Total Furniture		3,756.44
Total Fixed Assets		32,131.44

Figure 5.5
A Partial View of the Balance Sheet on March 31, 1997

Accumulated depreciation is not shown here because the account currently has a zero balance

4 Close all windows.

Having tackled prepaid asset and depreciable asset adjustments, you and Karen are now ready to move to the last adjustment category—adjusting unearned revenue.

ADJUSTING UNEARNED REVENUE

On March 6, 1997, Phoenix received $2,500 from its customer, Boston Stores. On this date, Boston Stores had no existing balance outstanding. As described in Chapter 3, Casey recorded this transaction by increasing Cash and decreasing Accounts Receivable. Casey later learned that $1,612.50 had subsequently been billed to Boston Stores on invoice 20008. Since the remaining $887.50 was an advance to future maintenance service, Casey correctly decided to reclassify it as unearned revenue, a liability, on March 31, 1997. Here's why. Cash has been received, but the maintenance service has not yet been fully provided. Thus, on March 31, you need to apply $1,612.50 to invoice 20008 and reclassify the balance of $887.50 to an unearned revenue account (a liability). When Phoenix performs the maintenance in a future period, Phoenix will create an invoice, decrease the liability, and increase sales revenue, all in the amount of $887.50.

To apply the advance to invoice 20008 at March 31, 1997:

1 Click **Activities** and then click **Receive Payments**.

2 Click **Prev** six times or until you come across the Boston Stores receipt of March 6, 1997.

3 Click **Auto Apply** as shown in Figure 5.6.

Figure 5.6

The Boston Stores Receive Payments Window Before Application

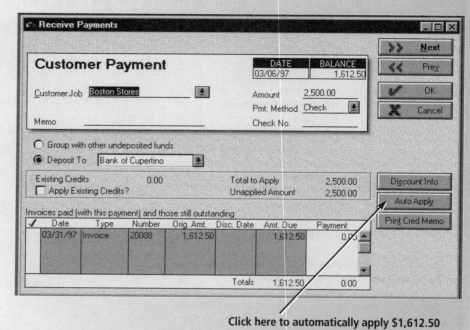

Click here to automatically apply $1,612.50 of the $2,500.00 in invoice 20008

4 Click **OK** to accept the application of $1,612.50 to invoice 20008. This leaves an unapplied amount of $887.50.

You now have to reclassify the balance as unearned revenue.

To reclassify the remaining balance as of March 31, 1997:

1 Click the **Acct** button on the icon bar, then click the **Account** button, then click **New** to create a new account.

2 Click **Other Current Liability** from the Type drop-down list.

3 Type **Unearned Revenue** in the Name edit box and click **OK**.

4 With the Unearned Revenue account selected click **Activities** then click **Use Register**.

5 Type the date, **March 31, 1997**, the payee, **Boston Stores**, and **887.50** in the Increase column of line one. Then select the account, **Accounts Receivable**, and type **To reclassify unearned revenue** in the memo section as shown in Figure 5.7. Note that the customer name needs to be entered to properly update Phoenix's accounts receivable account. The memo entry is not necessary, but it often helps for documentation purposes to add an explanation for the adjustment.

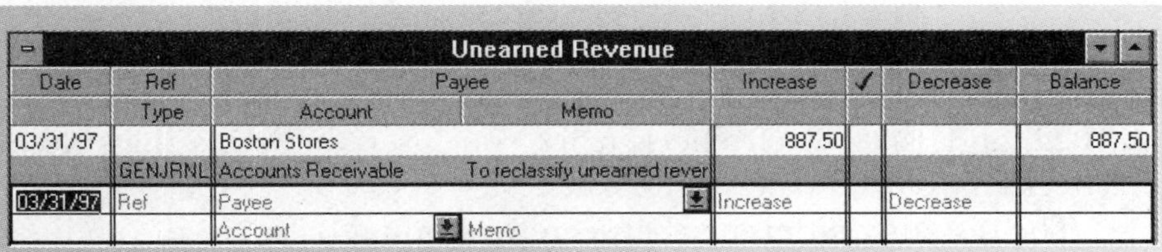

Figure 5.7
The Unearned Revenue Register

6 Click **Record**, then close the Unearned Revenue register and the Chart of Accounts.

7 Click **OK** on Receive Payments to record this change.

Together, you and Karen have now made all adjustments necessary except for those necessitated by the preparation of the bank reconciliation.

BANK RECONCILIATION

Every month the Bank of Cupertino sends Phoenix a checking account statement that lists all deposits received by the bank and all checks and payments that have cleared the bank as of the date of the statement. You and Karen examine the current bank statement, which indicates an ending balance of $85,206.87 as of February 28, 1997. You now turn your attention toward reconciling that balance with the balance reported by QuickBooks. You note that QuickBooks indicates an ending checking account balance of $77,988.06 at that same date and that most of the difference between these two amounts is probably attributable to "outstanding checks" that Phoenix has written but that the bank hasn't yet paid.

To reconcile the bank statement as of 2/28/97:

1 Click **Activities** and then click **Reconcile**.

2 Click **Bank of Cupertino** from the Account To Reconcile drop-down list.

3 Enter the bank reconciliation date of **2/28/97** in the Date fields shown in Figure 5.8. (Note the opening balance shown of $67,667.52. This is the sum of all previously cleared items in the register, which would equal the opening balance on the bank statement.)

4 Enter the ending balance, **$85,145.01**, and service charge, **65.00**.

5 Click **Bank Service Charges** from the Account drop-down list.

6 In the Deposits and Other Credits section, place a check next to all the deposits by clicking in the column to the left of every date except those deposits recorded in March. This check indicates that these deposits have been received by the bank.

7 In the Checks and Payments section, place a check next to all checks and payments having a January or February date except checks 1021, 1022, and 1023. Each check mark you insert indicates that these checks have been paid by the bank.

The resulting difference between the Ending Balance (the ending balance per the bank statement) and the Cleared Balance (the total of the opening balance plus the transactions you've marked) should now be 0 as shown in Figure 5.8.

trouble? If the difference is not 0, your account is not balanced for the period. The problem could be errors in your account register or errors made by the bank. Alternatively, you may not have checked the correct number of deposits or checks.

Figure 5.8
The Reconciliation Window

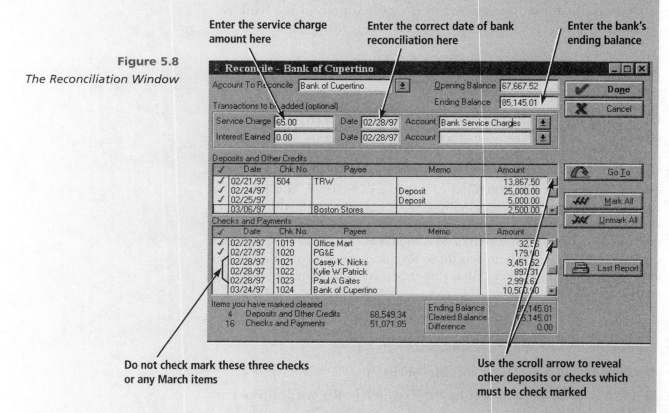

Enter the service charge amount here

Enter the correct date of bank reconciliation here

Enter the bank's ending balance

Do not check mark these three checks or any March items

Use the scroll arrow to reveal other deposits or checks which must be check marked

8 Click **Done** to complete the reconciliation.

trouble? If the difference is not 0, and you've clicked **Done,** you will see a Reconcile Adjustments window. Do not click OK to adjust the balance.

9 Click **Summary** in the Reconciliation Complete window to indicate you want a summary bank reconciliation report.

10 Enter **2/28/97** as the Statement Closing Date, then click **OK**.

11 Click **Print** in the Print Lists window, then click **Yes** in the Reconcile Report window if the report printed correctly.

The only adjustment created in this bank reconciliation was the recognition of bank service fees. QuickBooks automatically records this reduction in the checking account and increases bank service charges, an expense account. Once reconciled QuickBooks also inserts a check mark next to each transaction which has cleared the bank such as that shown in Figure 5.9.

These check marks indicate the item has cleared the bank

Date	Number	Payee	Account	Payment	✓	Deposit	Balance
02/27/97	1017	E-Max Realty	Accounts Payable	800.00	✓		85,575.99
02/27/97	1018	GTE	Accounts Payable	92.56	✓		85,483.43
02/27/97	1019	Office Mart	Accounts Payable	32.56	✓		85,450.87
02/27/97	1020	PG&E	Accounts Payable	179.00	✓		85,271.87
02/28/97			Bank Service Charges	65.00	✓		85,206.87
02/28/97	1021	Casey K. Nicks	-split-	3,421.14			81,785.73
02/28/97	1022	Kylie W Patrick	-split-	893.94			80,891.79
02/28/97	1023	Paul A Gates	-split-	2,968.73			77,923.06
03/06/97		Boston Stores	Accounts Receivable			2,500.00	80,423.06

Bank of Cupertino

Figure 5.9
The Check Register After Reconciliation

QuickBooks automatically records the service charge specified in the bank reconciliation

The new balance is $65 less than before the reconciliation due to bank service charges

END NOTE

You've now helped Karen record various adjustments to Phoenix Systems including accrued expenses, accrued revenues, expiration of prepaid and depreciable assets, reduction of unearned revenue, and one which reflected a completed bank reconciliation. You're almost ready to create Phoenix's financial statements.

practice

chapter

5

Chapter 5 Questions

1 Explain the register method of recording period end adjustments.

2 Give an example of an accrued revenue at Phoenix Systems other than the example given in this chapter. Explain how this example of accrued revenue would be adjusted using the register method.

3 Give an example of an accrued expense at Phoenix Systems other than the example given in this chapter. Explain how this example of accrued expense would be adjusted using the register method.

4 Give an example of an asset expiration at Phoenix Systems other than the example given in this chapter. Explain how this example would be adjusted using the register method.

5 Give an example of unearned revenue at Phoenix Systems and explain the process for period-end adjustments involving unearned revenue.

6 Explain how to access an account's register.

7 What Activities menu item do you use to start a bank reconciliation?

8 What account is typically used to record service charges?

9 When you've finished reconciling a bank account, what should be the difference between the ending balance and the cleared balance?

10 What information is included in the reconciliation report?

Chapter 5 Assignments

1 *Adding More Information to Phoenix Systems Consulting, Inc.*

Use phnx05cp.qbw from your Student Disk.

a. Add the following adjustments as of March 31, 1997:

(1) Interest revenue of $225 on short-term investments was earned, but not received.

(2) Loan interest expense of $275 on long-term borrowing was incurred, but not paid.

(3) Depreciation on furniture for the period amounted to $313.04.

(4) Prepaid rent of $800 expired during the period.

(5) A payment of $6,500 was received from Netscape and recorded January 14, 1997, $3,000 of this should be applied to invoice 20007. The balance represents advance payment for services to be performed at a later time.

   b. Prepare and print a summary bank reconciliation as of March 31, 1997, using the following information:

     (1) The bank statement balance as of March 31, 1997, was $70,915.27.

     (2) Bank service charges amounted to $75.00 during the month

     (3) All deposits listed in the QuickBooks Reconciliation window were received by the bank in March, except for one deposit for $40,000 dated March 31.

     (4) All checks and payments listed in the QuickBooks Reconciliation window were paid by the bank, except for checks 1032, 1033, and 1034.

   c. Prepare and print a standard balance sheet as of March 31, 1997, and a standard income statement for the quarter ended March 31, 1997.

2. *Using the South-Western Home Page for More Assignments or Cases*

If you have Internet access, go to the home page for this textbook at owen.swcollege.com.

Select the **Chapter 5** section, and complete the problem(s) your instructor assigns.

Go to
owen.swcollege.com

http://

Chapter 5 Case Problem: JENNINGS & ASSOCIATES—Adjustments

In Chapters 2, 3, and 4 you recreated Kelly Jennings' QuickBooks file as of March 31, 1997 before adjustments. Now it is time to enter those adjustments. Use kj05cp.qbw from your Student Disk. Note that additional transactions have been included in this file that were not included in Chapter 4, so do not use your completed kj04cp.qbw file.

1 Add the following adjustments:

   a. Interest revenue on short-term investments was earned, but not received. In February, $300 was earned, $159 in March.

   b. Loan interest expense of $80 on a vehicle loan was incurred in March, but not paid.

   c. Depreciation on computer equipment for February and March amounted to $145 and $290, respectively.

   d. Depreciation on furniture for February and March amounted to $41.67 for each month.

   e. Depreciation on vehicles in March amounted to $300.00.

   f. Prepaid liability insurance of $200 expired during February and again in March.

   g. Of the $2,000 received from Bob and Mary Schultz, $575 was earned during the month of March and billed via invoice 13. Apply this amount to the invoice and reclassify the balance as unearned revenue.

2 Prepare and print a summary bank reconciliation for the First Valley Savings & Loan account as of March 31, 1997, given the following information:

    a. The bank statement balance as of March 31, 1997 was $56,945.50.

    b. Bank service charges amounted to $45.00 during the month.

    c. All deposits listed in the QuickBooks Reconciliation window were received by the bank.

    d. All checks and payments listed in the QuickBooks Reconciliation window were paid by the bank, except for checks 1018 through 1020.

3 Prepare and print a standard balance sheet as of March 31, 1997, and a standard income statement for the quarter ended March 31, 1997.

chapter

6

Budgeting

In this chapter you will:

- **Create budgets for specific revenue accounts**

- **Create budgets for specific expense accounts**

- **Create a budgeted income statement**

- **Create specific budgets for assets, liabilities, and owners' equity accounts**

- **Create a budgeted balance sheet**

CASE: PHOENIX SYSTEMS CONSULTING, INC.
. . . .

Today Casey asks you and Karen to prepare financial statements for the first quarter of the year. He reminds you that he has already recorded all of the transactions for January through March, so you're ready to prepare the statements.

"But just preparing the statements is half the job," Karen points out. "You have to interpret these statements. How will you know if the company is doing well?"

Casey is quick to respond. "At the beginning of the year I used a spreadsheet program to establish budgets for the year. So I can compare the actual results shown in the statements you prepare with these budgets."

"Doesn't QuickBooks have a budgeting feature?" you ask.

"You're right!" exclaims Casey, " I didn't use that feature, but now that you mention it, I should have. Would the two of you mind entering my budget estimates into QuickBooks as well?"

"Not at all," you respond.

After Casey leaves, you explain to Karen that QuickBooks allows you to set up a budget for an account or for a customer within an account. To do this, you enter budget amounts for the income statement accounts or balance sheet accounts you wish to track.

"Are you able to track actual versus budgeted amounts?" Karen asks.

"Yes," you reply. "I'll show you how to use QuickBooks's budget reports to examine the budget by itself, as well as how to compare Phoenix's actual results to its budgeted amounts."

Karen has another question. "Can we create different budgets based on different assumptions in QuickBooks?"

"No," you answer. "QuickBooks allows you to have a different budget for different fiscal years, but you may have only one budget per fiscal year."

You explain that QuickBooks allows you to set up budgets for specific accounts within financial statements or for all specific financial statements. While it is easier to budget for specific accounts, it might be more useful to prepare a budgeted income statement or budgeted balance sheet.

To begin, you suggest that Karen print Casey's spreadsheet budget and then the two of you establish the monthly budget for revenues.

BUDGETS FOR SPECIFIC REVENUES
. . . .

QuickBooks provides a set-up window to enter budget information. In this window you specify fiscal year, account, customer, and/or class and the corresponding amounts for each month. As you fill in this information, you are setting up a budget for a single account, such as a balance sheet or an income statement account. If you also choose a customer:job or a class, you can set up a budget for that account and for that customer:job or class.

"I remember entering customer:job information in QuickBooks, but what are classes?" asks Karen.

"Classes are categories QuickBooks provides to help you group data into departments, product lines, locations, and the like."

"Do we need to set up budgets for customers or classes?" asks Karen.

"Casey's budget isn't that detailed," you respond. "We'll enter information for accounts only."

Karen also asks about QuickBooks's use of the term *income* instead of *revenues* for products and services. You explain that although revenues is the traditional accounting term for these items, QuickBooks has chosen to classify them as "income" in the type section of the chart of accounts.

To create budgets for specific revenues:

1 Open QuickBooks if it is not already open, then open phnx06.qbw from your Student Disk.

2 Click **Activities** and then click **Set Up Budgets**.

3 Click the appropriate arrow to set the Budget for Fiscal Year to **1997** as shown in Figure 6.1.

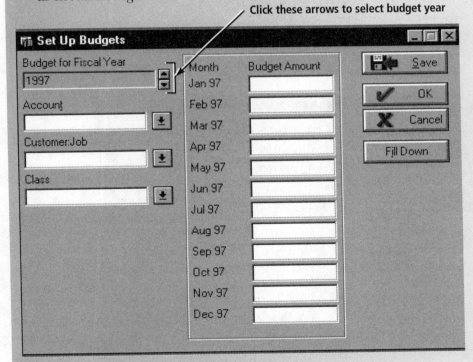

Figure 6.1
The Set Up Budgets Window

4 Select **Computer Add-ons** from the Account drop-down list.

5 Type **1000** in the Jan 97 edit box, then click the **Fill Down** button.

6 Type **0.0%** in the Fill Down edit box to indicate no incremental increases, as shown in Figure 6.2. Then click **OK** in the Fill Down window. You have now established a budget for the Computer Add-ons account.

Figure 6.2
Fill Down Window

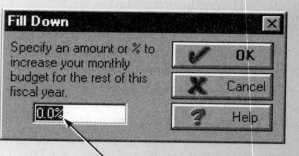

Type 0.0% here to indicate no increase in monthly budget amounts

7 Select **Computer Sales** from the Account drop-down list. *Note:* By selecting another account from the Set Up Budgets window, the information just entered is automatically saved. You do not need to click the Save button or the OK button to save this data.

8 Type **15000** in the Jan 97 edit box, then click the **Fill Down** button.

9 Type **5000** in the Fill Down edit box to indicate a flat 5,000 incremental increase each month, then click **OK** in the Fill Down window.

10 The resulting budget is shown in Figure 6.3.

These budget amounts result from filling down January's
15,000 with an increment of an additional $5,000 per month

Figure 6.3
Budget for Computer Sales

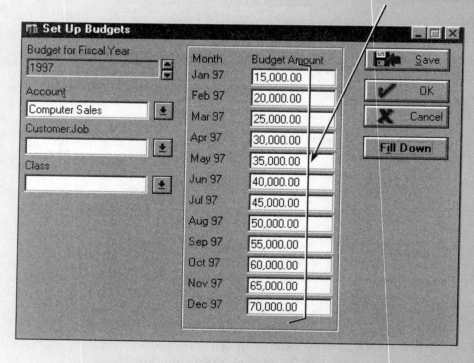

11 Select **Consulting Income** from the Account drop-down list.

12 Type **3000** in the Jan 97 edit box, then click the **Fill Down** button.

13 Type **0.0%** in the Fill Down edit box, then click **OK**.

14 Select **Maintenance & Repairs** from the Account drop-down list.

15 Type **3000** in the Jan 97 edit box, then click the **Fill Down** button.

16 Type **10.0%** in the Fill Down edit box to increment each month's budget, as shown in Figure 6.4, then click **OK**.

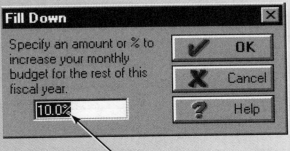

Enter 10.0% here to create a monthly incremental increase of 10%

Figure 6.4
Fill Down Window for Maintenance & Repairs

Now you're ready to set up budgets for specific expenses.

BUDGETS FOR SPECIFIC EXPENSES

The budget for Phoenix System's cost of goods sold or cost of sales depends on product sales. Casey estimated that product cost should amount to approximately 70% of sales. Thus, as budgeted sales increase, so should budgeted cost of sales. Karen recalls that in January you set up the budget to include $1,000 for Computer Add-ons and $15,000 for Computer Sales. Thus, expected cost of sales should be 70% of the total January sales of $16,000, or $11,200. Each month thereafter, Casey expects the combination of these two accounts to increase $5,000. Accordingly, the related costs of sales should increase monthly by 70%, or $3,500.

Casey expects payroll expenses, the largest budgeted expense item for Phoenix, to remain constant at $12,000 for six months and then increase to a constant $13,000 for the remaining six months. Depreciation expense, based on the fixed asset acquisitions, are recorded quarterly and are expected to be $700 in March, $800 in June, $1,000 in September, and $1,100 in December. Additional expenses may be budgeted at a later time.

To create a budget for specific expenses:

1 Select **Cost of Goods Sold** from the Account drop-down list.
   trouble? Although this account does not have the word "expense" in its title and does have a cost of goods sold account type, it is an expense account.

2 Type **16000 * 0.70** in the Jan 97 edit box, as shown in Figure 6.5, press [**Enter**], then click the **Fill Down** button.

Figure 6.5
*Using the Calculator During
Budget Set Up*

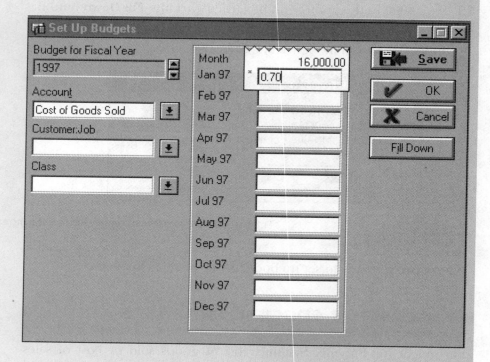

3 Type **3500** (the result of multiplying 5,000 by .70) in the Fill Down edit box to increment each month's budget, then click **OK**.

4 Select **Payroll Expenses** from the Account drop-down list.

5 Type **12000** in the Jan 97 edit box, then click the **Fill Down** button.

6 Type **0.0%** in the Fill Down edit box to complete each month's budget, then click **OK**.

7 Edit the months of July through December 1997, changing the amounts from 12,000 to **13,000**.

8 Select **Depreciation Expense** from the Account drop-down list .

9 Type **700** in the March edit box, **800** in the June edit box, **1000** in the September edit box, and **1100** in the December edit box. You're skipping months because depreciation is recorded quarterly.

10 Click **OK** to save your budget changes and close the Set Up Budgets window.

Now that Karen has entered budgetary information for several specific income statement accounts, she is curious to see a complete budget. Thus, she will create and print a budgeted income statement for the first quarter of 1997.

To create and print a budgeted income statement:

1 Click **File**, then click **Preferences**, then click the **Reports & Graphs** icon.

2 Be sure that the check box labeled Display Customize Report window automatically, located at the bottom of the Preferences window, is checked. If it is, click **OK**; if it is not, click in the check box, then click **OK**.

3 Click **Reports**, then click **Budget Reports**, then click **P&L Budget Overview**.

4 Enter **1/1/97** and **3/31/97** as the from and to dates respectively in the Customize Report window, then click **OK**.

5 Click the **Header/Footer** button on the Report toolbar and change the report title to Budgeted Income Statement, then click **OK** in the Format Header/Footer window.

6 Click the **Print** button on the Report toolbar.

7 Click **Portrait orientation**, click the **Fit to One Page Wide** check box, then click **Print** to print the report. Your report should look like Figure 6.6.

	Jan '97	Feb '97	Mar '97	Total Jan–Mar '97
Ordinary Income/Expense				
Income				
Computer Add-ons	1,000.00	1,000.00	1,000.00	3,000.00
Computer Sales	15,000.00	20,000.00	25,000.00	60,000.00
Consulting Income	3,000.00	3,000.00	3,000.00	9,000.00
Maintenance & Repairs	3,000.00	3,300.00	3,630.00	9,930.00
Total Income	22,000.00	27,300.00	32,630.00	81,930.00
Cost of Goods Sold				
Cost of Goods Sold	11,200.00	14,700.00	18,200.00	44,100.00
Total COGS	11,200.00	14,700.00	18,200.00	44,100.00
Gross Profit	10,800.00	12,600.00	14,430.00	37,830.00
Expense				
Depreciation Expense			700.00	700.00
Payroll Expense	12,000.00	12,000.00	12,000.00	36,000.00
Total Expense	12,000.00	12,000.00	12,700.00	36,700.00
Net Ordinary Income	-1,200.00	600.00	1,730.00	1,130.00
Net Income	-1,200.00	600.00	1,730.00	1,130.00

Figure 6.6
Budgeted Income Statement for the First Quarter of 1997

8 Review the Budgeted Income Statement, then close the Report window.

"Are we ready to compare our budget with actual results?" asks Karen.

"Not yet," you reply. "We still have to enter budgeted data for assets, liabilities, and owners' equity."

BUDGET FOR ASSETS, LIABILITIES, AND OWNERS' EQUITY

You explain to Karen that creating specific budgets for assets, liabilities, and owners' equity accounts is not a simple task. First, you cannot complete this task until the budget for revenues and expenses has been established. This is due to the relationship that exists between net income and retained earnings. Budgeted retained earnings is dependent on net income/net loss. That is, budgeted retained earnings must be increased by monthly net income and decreased by monthly net losses, if any.

Second, budgets for accounts receivable are dependent on sales, while budgets for inventory and accounts payable are dependent on cost of sales and projected sales. Budgeted accumulated depreciation accounts are increased by monthly depreciation expenses. Fortunately for you and Karen, Casey has already created this budget in his spreadsheet program.

Karen suggests that you complete this task one step at a time—first entering the budget for assets, then the budget for liabilities, followed by the budget for owners' equity.

You agree with her suggestion and remind her that the budget amounts for these accounts are the ending balance expected for each month.

To create a budget for assets:

1 Click **Activities** and then click **Set Up Budgets**.

2 Click the appropriate arrow to set the Budget for Fiscal Year to 1997.

3 Select **Bank of Cupertino** from the Account drop-down list.

4 Enter the projected budget balances as shown in Figure 6.7.

Figure 6.7

Budget Balances for the Bank of Cupertino Account

Month	Budget Amount
Jan 97	26,300.00
Feb 97	27,900.00
Mar 97	33,330.00
Apr 97	34,623.00
May 97	38,815.30
Jun 97	16,946.83
Jul 97	7,461.51
Aug 97	12,307.66
Sep 97	20,438.43
Oct 97	14,812.28
Nov 97	10,393.52
Dec 97	18,252.88

5 Select **Short-term Investments** from the Account drop-down list.

6 Enter the projected budget balances as shown in Figure 6.8.

Month	Budget Amount
Jan 97	25,000.00
Feb 97	34,000.00
Mar 97	50,000.00
Apr 97	17,000.00
May 97	3,000.00
Jun 97	12,000.00
Jul 97	14,000.00
Aug 97	15,000.00
Sep 97	17,000.00
Oct 97	18,000.00
Nov 97	10,000.00
Dec 97	2,000.00

Figure 6.8

Budget Balances for the Short-Term Investments Account

7 Select **Accounts Receivable** from the Account drop-down list.

8 Type **15000** in the Jan 97 edit box, then click the **Fill Down** button.

9 Type **5000** in the Fill Down edit box to increment each month's budget, then click **OK** in the Fill Down edit box.

10 Select **Inventory Asset** from the Account drop-down list.

11 Type **20000** in the Jan 97 edit box, then click the **Fill Down** button.

12 Type **10000** in the Fill Down edit box to increment each month's budget, then click **OK** in the Fill Down edit box.

13 Select **Computer Equipment:Cost** from the Account drop-down list.

14 Enter projected budget balances as shown in Figure 6.9.

Month	Budget Amount
Jan 97	0.00
Feb 97	7,000.00
Mar 97	30,000.00
Apr 97	35,000.00
May 97	35,000.00
Jun 97	35,000.00
Jul 97	40,000.00
Aug 97	40,000.00
Sep 97	40,000.00
Oct 97	40,000.00
Nov 97	40,000.00
Dec 97	40,000.00

Figure 6.9

Budget Balances for the Computer Equipment:Cost Account

15 Select **Furniture:Cost** from the Account drop-down list.

16 Type **3500** in the Jan 97 edit box, then click the **Fill Down** button.

17 Type **0.0%** in the Fill Down edit box to replicate the same amount for all months, then click **OK**.

18 Select **Computer Equipment:Accumulated Depreciation** from the Account drop-down list.

19 Type **–400** in the Mar, April, and May 97 edit boxes. Since depreciation is recorded only quarterly, the Accumulated Depreciation account will show the same amount for each of these three months.

20 Type **–800** in the Jun, Jul, and Aug 97 edit boxes.

21 Type **–1300** in the Sep, Oct, and Nov 97 edit boxes.

22 Type **–1800** in the Dec 97 edit box.

23 Select **Furniture:Accumulated Depreciation** from the Account drop-down list.

24 Enter the projected budget balances as shown in Figure 6.10.

Figure 6.10

Budget Balances for the Accumulated Depreciation Furniture Account

Month	Budget Amount
Jan 97	
Feb 97	
Mar 97	-300.00
Apr 97	-300.00
May 97	-300.00
Jun 97	-700.00
Jul 97	-700.00
Aug 97	-700.00
Sep 97	-1,200.00
Oct 97	-1,200.00
Nov 97	-1,200.00
Dec 97	-1,800.00

Karen comments that budgeted liabilities are also related to operating activities. For example, accounts payable will vary with projected purchases for inventory, and payroll tax liabilities will vary with employment and the frequency of tax deposits. Likewise, sales tax liabilities will vary with sales of taxable items and the frequency of tax deposits.

Short-term and long-term debt will vary with financing requirements and cash flows. Slow cash flow from increasing accounts receivable and inventory will require more financing and must be planned early. Karen is happy to see that Casey has anticipated this need; he has arranged for future financing and has included it in his budget.

Casey's budget reveals a consistent pattern of increasing accounts payable to support planned inventory purchases. He plans to pay payroll and sales taxes quarterly. He believes that short-term debt will remain constant over the year, while he expects long-term financing to grow steadily.

With this background information, you are ready to create a budget for liabilities.

To create a budget for liabilities:

1 Select **Accounts Payable** from the Account drop-down list.

2 Type **10000** in the Jan 97 edit box, then click the **Fill Down** button.

3 Type **5000** in the Fill Down edit box to increment each month's budget, then click **OK**.

4 Select **Payroll Liabilities** from the Account drop-down list.

5 Enter the projected budget balances as shown in Figure 6.11.

Month	Budget Amount
Jan 97	4,000.00
Feb 97	8,000.00
Mar 97	12,000.00
Apr 97	4,000.00
May 97	8,000.00
Jun 97	12,000.00
Jul 97	4,000.00
Aug 97	8,000.00
Sep 97	12,000.00
Oct 97	4,000.00
Nov 97	8,000.00
Dec 97	12,000.00

Figure 6.11

Budget Balances for the Payroll Liabilities Account

6 Select **Sales Tax Payable** from the Account drop-down list.

7 Enter the projected budget balances as shown in Figure 6.12.

8 Select **Short-term Debt** from the Account drop-down list.

9 Type **10000** in the Feb 97 edit box, then click the **Fill Down** button.

10 Type **0.0%** in the Fill Down edit box to replicate the same amount for all remaining months, then click **OK**.

11 Select **Long-term Debt** from the Account drop-down list.

Figure 6.12

Budget Balances for the Sales Tax Payable Account

Month	Budget Amount
Jan 97	2,000.00
Feb 97	5,000.00
Mar 97	8,000.00
Apr 97	3,000.00
May 97	6,000.00
Jun 97	9,000.00
Jul 97	4,000.00
Aug 97	7,000.00
Sep 97	10,000.00
Oct 97	5,000.00
Nov 97	8,000.00
Dec 97	11,000.00

12 Enter the projected budget balances as shown in Figure 6.13.

Figure 6.13

Budget Balances for the Long-Term Debt Account

Month	Budget Amount
Jan 97	0.00
Feb 97	10,000.00
Mar 97	55,000.00
Apr 97	55,000.00
May 97	50,000.00
Jun 97	45,000.00
Jul 97	68,400.00
Aug 97	78,100.00
Sep 97	90,000.00
Oct 97	105,000.00
Nov 97	90,000.00
Dec 97	85,000.00

You comment that this budgeting process is more complicated than you thought it would be. Karen agrees, but she assures you that creating the budget for owners' equity won't be as difficult, because owners' equity should increase or decrease by the amount of net income.

"That makes sense," you agree, "but what about other owners' equity transactions, such as additional investments and dividends?"

"I think we would budget them just like other accounts, but Casey's budget doesn't include these items," Karen replies.

"Good. Let's just figure the balance in Retained Earnings each month as being the prior month's balance plus net income or minus net losses. We can't forget Capital Stock either; although it didn't change during the year, it still has to be budgeted."

To create a budget for owners' equity:

1 Select **Capital Stock** from the Account drop-down list.

2 Type **75000** in the Jan 97 edit box, then click the **Fill Down** button.

3 Type **0.0%** in the Fill Down edit box to replicate the same amount for all remaining months, then click **OK**.

4 Select **Retained Earnings** from the Account drop-down list.

5 Enter the projected budget balances as shown in Figure 6.14, then click **OK** in the Set Up Budgets window to accept the budget amounts for Retained Earnings, and close the window.

Month	Budget Amount
Jan 97	-1,200.00
Feb 97	-600.00
Mar 97	1,130.00
Apr 97	-2,577.00
May 97	-4,384.70
Jun 97	-10,053.17
Jul 97	-12,938.49
Aug 97	-13,792.34
Sep 97	-13,561.57
Oct 97	-10,187.72
Nov 97	-4,606.48
Dec 97	2,152.88

Figure 6.14
Budget Balances for the Retained Earnings Account

Now that you have completed entering the budget information, you will want to see how a quarterly report will look. To keep it manageable, Karen suggests that you create and print only the budgeted balance sheet as of the end of the first three months of the year.

To create and print a budgeted balance sheet:

1 Click **Reports**, then click **Budget Reports**, then click **Balance Sheet Budget Overview**.

2 Enter **1/1/97** and **3/31/97** as the from and to dates, respectively, in the Customize Report window, then click **OK**.

3 Click the **Print** button on the Report toolbar.

4 Click the **Portrait** orientation option button, click the **Fit to One Page Wide** check box, and then click **OK** to print the report shown in Figure 6.15.

Figure 6.15 *Budgeted Balance Sheet for the First Quarter of 1997*

	Jan 31, '97	Feb 28, '97	Mar 31, '97
ASSETS			
Current Assets			
Checking/Savings			
Bank of Cupertino	26,300.00	27,900.00	33,330.00
Short-term Investments	25,000.00	34,000.00	50,000.00
Total Checking/Savings	51,300.00	61,900.00	83,330.00
Accounts Receivable			
Accounts Receivable	15,000.00	20,000.00	25,000.00
Total Accounts Receivable	15,000.00	20,000.00	25,000.00
Other Current Assets			
Inventory Asset	20,000.00	30,000.00	40,000.00
Total Other Current Assets	20,000.00	30,000.00	40,000.00
Total Current Assets	86,300.00	111,900.00	148,330.00
Fixed Assets			
Computer Equipment			
Cost	0.00	7,000.00	30,000.00
Accumulated Depreciation			−400.00
Total Computer Equipment	0.00	7,000.00	29,600.00
Furniture			
Cost	3,500.00	3,500.00	3,500.00
Accumulated Depreciation			−300.00
Total Furniture	3,500.00	3,500.00	3,200.00
Total Fixed Assets	3,500.00	10,500.00	32,800.00
TOTAL ASSETS	**89,800.00**	**122,400.00**	**181,130.00**
LIABILITIES & EQUITY			
Liabilities			
Current Liabilities			
Accounts Payable			
Accounts Payable	10,000.00	15,000.00	20,000.00
Total Accounts Payable	10,000.00	15,000.00	20,000.00
Other Current Liabilities			
Payroll Liabilities	4,000.00	8,000.00	12,000.00
Sales Tax Payable	2,000.00	5,000.00	8,000.00
Short-term Debt		10,000.00	10,000.00
Total Other Current Liabilities	6,000.00	23,000.00	30,000.00
Total Current Liabilities	16,000.00	38,000.00	50,000.00
Long-term Liabilities			
Long-term Debt	0.00	10,000.00	55,000.00
Total Long-term Liabilities	0.00	10,000.00	55,000.00
Total Liabilities	16,000.00	48,000.00	105,000.00
Equity			
Capital Stock	75,000.00	75,000.00	75,000.00
Retained Earnings	-1,200.00	-600.00	1,130.00
Total Equity	73,800.00	74,400.00	76,130.00
TOTAL LIABILITIES & EQUITY	**89,800.00**	**122,400.00**	**181,130.00**

5 Review the Budget Report, then close the Report window.

END NOTE
. . . .

You and Karen have now entered all budgetary information for the first quarter of 1997. Casey can make changes to the budget at any time if additional information becomes available, and QuickBooks will automatically update any related budget report. In Chapter 7 you will generate the financial statements Casey requested, so he can compare the budget with actual results.

practice

chapter

6

Chapter 6 Questions

1 Explain how the budgeting process is accomplished in QuickBooks.

2 Can multiple budgets be created in QuickBooks? Explain.

3 Explain how the Fill Down feature helps in creating QuickBooks budgets.

4 Does the Fill Down feature allow you to increase or decrease by specific dollar amounts only? Explain.

5 Explain the typical relationship between cost of goods sold and sales in the budgeting process and how this information is included in the QuickBooks budgeting process.

6 Compare the process of budgeting revenues and expenses with the process of budgeting assets, liabilities, and owners' equity and how this information is included in the QuickBooks budgeting process.

7 Explain the typical relationship between accumulated depreciation and depreciation expense in the budgeting process and how this information is included in the QuickBooks budgeting process.

8 Which menus are used to create budget reports in QuickBooks?

9 Describe how you use the calculator feature that is built into QuickBooks for the budgeting process.

10 Explain the typical relationship between retained earnings and net income/loss in the budgeting process and how this information is included in the QuickBooks budgeting process.

Chapter 6 Assignments

1 *Modifying Budgets for Phoenix Systems, Inc.*

Casey has revised his original budget. He asks you to modify the QuickBooks file accordingly. Use the phnx06cp.qbw data file from your Student Disk to make the following changes. Then create a budgeted income statement and budgeted balance sheet for the first quarter ending March 31, 1997.

a. Computer sales are expected to be $13,000 in Jan '97 and increase $6,000 each month thereafter.

b. The budget for cash (checking account Bank of Cupertino) will change as per Figure 6.16.

c. Accounts payable are expected to be $10,000 at the end of January 1997, increase 30% in February 1997, and then remain constant for 3 months. Thereafter Casey expects accounts payable to increase 100% in May 1997 and continue to increase by $10,000 per month throughout the remainder of the year.

d. Casey changed the budget for retained earnings as shown in Figure 6.17.

2 **Using the South-Western Home Page for More Assignments or Cases**

If you have Internet access, go to the home page for this textbook at owen.swcollege.com

Select the **Chapter 6** section, and complete the problem(s) your instructor assigns.

Go to
owen.swcollege.com

Figure 6.16

Revised Budget Amounts for Cash

Month	Budget Amount
Jan 97	24,300.00
Feb 97	22,900.00
Mar 97	23,330.00
Apr 97	20,623.00
May 97	34,815.30
Jun 97	20,946.83
Jul 97	20,461.51
Aug 97	35,307.66
Sep 97	54,438.43
Oct 97	60,812.28
Nov 97	69,393.52
Dec 97	91,252.88

Figure 6.17

Revised Budget Amounts for Retained Earnings

Month	Budget Amount
Jan 97	-3,200.00
Feb 97	-3,600.00
Mar 97	-1,870.00
Apr 97	-4,577.00
May 97	-4,384.70
Jun 97	-7,053.17
Jul 97	-5,938.49
Aug 97	-1,792.34
Sep 97	4,438.43
Oct 97	14,812.28
Nov 97	28,393.52
Dec 97	44,152.88

Chapter 6 Case Problem: JENNINGS & ASSOCIATES—Budgets

Kelly Jennings is anxious to compare her operating, investing, and financing activities with corresponding budgeted amounts. To do this she must first enter her budget into QuickBooks.

Use kj06cp.qbw from your Student Disk. (*Note:* Transactions that were not included in Chapter 5 have been added to this file. Do not use your completed kj05cp.qbw file.)

1 Create and print a budgeted income statement for the first quarter of 1997 assuming the following information:

   a. Fee income of $14,000 is expected in the first month, increasing by 10% each month thereafter.
   b. Depreciation expense of $200 per month is expected.
   c. Payroll expenses of $10,000 are expected for January 1997, and then remain at $14,000 for each month thereafter.
   d. Rent expense is anticipated at $700 per month.

2 Create and print a budgeted balance sheet for the first quarter of 1997 assuming the following information: (Remember that balance sheet accounts represent balances at the end of each month. Thus amounts provided are not monthly increases but ending balances.)

   a. Cash in the First Valley Savings & Loan account is budgeted at $2,000 at the end of January 1997 and $50,000 at the end of February 1997. Thereafter it is expected to decline $5,000 each month.
   b. Cash in the Union Bank checking account is budgeted as shown in Figure 6.18.

Figure 6.18

*Budget for Union Bank
Checking Account*

Month	Budget Amount
Jan 97	3,840.00
Feb 97	26,600.00
Mar 97	29,227.20
Apr 97	35,354.86
May 97	45,129.16
Jun 97	56,710.43
Jul 97	70,474.51
Aug 97	86,014.24
Sep 97	104,141.10
Oct 97	124,886.97
Nov 97	148,506.12
Dec 97	175,277.33

c. Accounts Receivable is budgeted at $12,000 at the end of January 1997 and is expected to increase at the rate of 12% per month.

d. Inventory is expected to average $2,500 each month.

e. Computer Equipment:Cost is budgeted for $4,000 in January 1997, $8,000 in February 1997, and $14,000 for the remainder of the year.

f. Computer Equipment:Accumulated Depreciation is budgeted for –$1,000 in January 1997 and is expected to change by –$175 each subsequent month.

g. Furniture:Cost is budgeted to remain at $2,500 for the year.

h. Furniture:Accumulated Depreciation is budgeted for $500 in January 1997, increasing $25 each month for the rest of the year.

i. Accounts Payable is budgeted at $8,000 in January 1997, increasing $1,000 each month thereafter.

j. Payroll Liabilities are budgeted at $3,500 in January 1997, $8,000 in February 1997, $10,000 in March 1997, and are expected to remain at $8,000 each month throughout the rest of the year.

k. The Bank of San Martin long-term liability is budgeted at $5,000 per month for the year.

l. Capital Stock is budgeted for $3,590 in January 1997 and should remain at $73,590 for February through December 1997.

m. Retained Earnings began the year at $2,150 and is adjusted monthly by the amount of net income or loss. (*Hint:* Examine the budgeted income statement you prepared in Item 1 above to identify the budgeted net income or loss each month. Add net income to [or subtract net loss from] the prior month's ending retained earnings to calculate each month's ending retained earnings.)

chapter

7

Reporting Business Activities

In this chapter you will:

- Create an end-of-period income statement and a budgeted vs. actual income statement

- Create an end-of-period balance sheet and a budgeted vs. actual balance sheet

- Create graphs to illustrate sales and income and expenses

- Create graphs to illustrate receivables and payables

- Create additional reports for sales, purchases, and inventory, and for accounts receivable and accounts payable aging

CASE: PHOENIX SYSTEMS CONSULTING, INC.

Now that you have entered the budget information for Phoenix System's first fiscal year and have made all first quarter operating, investing, and financing transactions as well as adjustments, you are ready to prepare Phoenix's first quarter financial statements. Casey has asked you and Karen to prepare these statements and to provide any additional information that will help him better understand Phoenix's financial performance. So you decide that in addition to the financial statements, you will give Casey the related supporting schedules and graphs that QuickBooks can so easily create.

You decide to prepare an income statement, a balance sheet, an accounts receivable and accounts payable schedule, and an inventory status report. To further enhance Casey's financial analysis of the business, you also decide to prepare one graph showing revenues and expenses and another showing the aging of accounts receivable and payable.

"The report and graph features of QuickBooks are quite extensive," you explain to Karen. "You can customize each report by adding percentages, hiding cents, changing report titles, and modifying the page layout."

"Can we also compare the current quarter's results with the budget we just created?" asks Karen.

"Absolutely!" you confirm. "Now that we have created the budget in QuickBooks, we can easily generate a report comparing our budgeted activity with our actual results. We can also produce graphs to help Casey or other users of this information visually evaluate the financial results."

"Sounds like QuickBooks saves hours of work," Karen remarks. "Let's get started."

CREATING INCOME STATEMENTS

You decide to create one income statement for the period without examining each month separately, because adjustments were made only as of March 31.

You explain to Karen that QuickBooks enables you to create reports for any period you desire. It also lets you create separate columns for a time segment—such as a day, a week, four weeks, a month, a quarter, and so on—within each period. You decide that this income statement will report totals only, because adjustments were made only once in the quarter. Then at the end of the fiscal year, you'll create an income statement report for the year with separate columns for each quarter.

"Do we have to go through this customization effort every time?" Karen asks.

"No, " you reply. "QuickBooks has a Memorize feature that can "memorize" or retain the customization—what columns we want, what period, what layout, and so on. That way the next time we want a similar report, it will be available from a memorized report list."

To create the first quarter income statement:

1 Open QuickBooks, if it is not already open, then open phnx07.qbw from your Student Disk.

2 Click **Reports**, **Profit & Loss**, then **Standard**.

3 Change the report dates to read from **1/1/97** to **3/31/97** in the Cus-tomize Report window, click the **% of Income** check box, and then click **OK**.

4 Click the **Format** button, then click the **Show All Numbers Without Cents** check box, then click **OK**.

5 Use the **Header/Footer** button to change the Report Title to **Income Statement,** to make the Header a Left Page Layout, and to alter the Subtitle to **for the three months ended March 31, 1997**, then click **OK** in the Format Report window.

6 Click the **Print** button, then click **Print** in the Print Reports window to print the report shown in Figure 7.1.

7 Click the **Memorize** button, then click **OK** to retain this customized report as Income Statement.

8 Close all windows.

Notice in this report that 79% of the company's revenue comes from computer sales and 10% from maintenance and repairs. This percent column reports what percentage of total revenue (what QuickBooks calls total income) each item is. Cost of goods sold at 58% and payroll expenses at 33% are the company's largest costs as a percentage of total revenue. Notice also that Phoenix's profit margin ratio (net income divided by total revenue) is 8%.

Now you need to compare Phoenix's budgeted operating activity with its actual operating results. You tell Karen that you can customize a budgeted versus actual report to include only selected information and to change its layout from the default format that QuickBooks provides.

To create a budgeted and actual income statement comparison:

1 Click **Reports**, **Budget Reports**, then click **P & L Budget vs. Actual**.

2 Change the report dates from **1/1/97** to **3/31/97** in the Customize Report window.

3 Select **Quarter** from the Columns drop-down edit box.

4 Make sure that all check boxes—**Show Actuals**, **and Difference**, and **and % of Budget**—are checked, then click **OK**.

5 Click the **Format** button, then click the **Show All Numbers Without Cents** check box, then click **OK**.

Figure 7.1

A Customized Income Statement for Phoenix with a Percent of Income Column

Phoenix Software 07
Income Statement
for the three months ended March 31, 1997

	Jan–Mar '97	% of Income
Ordinary Income/Expense		
Income		
Computer Add-ons	3,100	3%
Computer Sales	80,950	79%
Consulting Income	7,800	8%
Maintenance & Repairs	10,625	10%
Parts Income	150	0%
Total Income	102,625	100%
Cost of Goods Sold		
Cost of Goods Sold	59,170	58%
Total COGS	59,170	58%
Gross Profit	43,455	42%
Expense		
Bank Service Charges	185	0%
Depreciation Expense	688	1%
Insurance		
Liability Insurance	346	0%
Total Insurance	346	0%
Interest Expense		
Loan Interest	525	1%
Total Interest Expense	525	1%
Office Supplies	650	1%
Payroll Expenses	34,123	33%
Rent	2,400	2%
Telephone	328	0%
Utilities		
Gas and Electric	619	1%
Total Utilities	619	1%
Total Expenses	39,864	39%
Net Ordinary Income	3,591	3%
Other Income/Expense		
Other Income		
Investment Income	3,500	3%
Interest Revenue	725	1%
Total Other Income	4,225	4%
Net Other Income	4,225	4%
Net Income	**7,816**	**8%**

6 Click the **Print** button. Make sure the **Fit report to one page wide** check box is checked, then click **Print** in the Print Reports window to print the report shown in Figure 7.2.

7 Close all windows.

Figure 7.2

A Budgeted vs. Actual Income Statement for Phoenix

Phoenix Software 07
P&L Budget Comparison
January through March 1997

	Jan–Mar '97	Budget	$ Over Budget	% of Budget
Ordinary Income/Expense				
Income				
Computer Add-ons	3,100	3,000	100	103%
Computer Sales	80,950	60,000	20,950	135%
Consulting Income	7,800	9,000	–1,200	87%
Maintenance & Repairs	10,625	9,930	695	107%
Parts Income	150	0	150	100%
Total Income	102,625	81,930	20,695	125%
Cost of Goods Sold				
Cost of Goods Sold	59,170	44,100	15,070	134%
Total COGS	59,170	44,100	15,070	134%
Gross Profit	43,455	37,830	5,625	115%
Expense				
Bank Service Charges	185			
Depreciation Expense	688	700	–12	98%
Insurance				
Liability Insurance	346			
Total Insurance	346			
Interest Expense				
Loan Interest	525			
Total Interest Expense	525			
Office Supplies	650			
Payroll Expenses	34,123	36,000	–1,877	95%
Rent	2,400			
Telephone	328			
Utilities				
Gas and Electric	619			
Total Utilities	619			
Total Expense	39,864	36,700	3,164	109%
Net Ordinary Income	3,591	1,130	2,461	318%
Other Income/Expense				
Other Income				
Investment Income	3,500			
Interest Revenue	725			
Total Other Income	4,225			
Net Other Income	4,225			
Net Income	**7,816**	**1,130**	**6,686**	**692%**

You and Karen go to Casey's office with both reports in hand. As you explain the budget comparison to him, his eyes grow large and focus on the % of Budget column.

"Wow!" he exclaims. "A 692% net income! We're doing great!"

"Not exactly," Karen interrupts. "The 692% figure means that your actual net income is 692% greater than the amount you budgeted. But since you budgeted net income of only $1,130, any deviation in actual results from that small budgeted number is significantly magnified in percentage terms."

Karen continues to explain that the company's revenues were 125% higher than planned; but that cost of goods sold was 134% higher than planned. Because Casey is somewhat uncertain as to how to interpret this information, you suggest that analyzing the balance sheet would be likely to help him gain a more complete picture of how well the company has performed.

CREATING BALANCE SHEETS

You return to your office to create the balance sheets Casey needs for the first quarter. You explain to Karen that QuickBooks can prepare balance sheets for any accounting period you specify. Since Casey wants results from the first quarter of the fiscal year of Phoenix's activities, the two of you start by preparing a standard balance sheet. You want to keep the report simple—you'll include the main accounts from the chart of accounts and collapse the subaccounts into their main accounts. Later you'll customize the balance sheet to include a percentage column, and then you'll create a budgeted and actual balance sheet comparison—taking advantage of the budget work you did previously.

To create a standard balance sheet:

1 Click **Reports**, **Balance Sheet**, then **Standard**.

2 Change the report dates from **1/1/97** to **3/31/97**, then click **OK**.

3 Click the **Print** button, then click **Print** in the Print Reports window to print the report shown in Figure 7.3.

trouble? Notice that QuickBooks includes a line item called "Net Income" in the (Owners') Equity section. Standard accounting practice does not allow inclusion of such an income statement category in a balance sheet. Usually this net income is included in the Retained Earnings account.

Figure 7.3

Standard Balance Sheet for Phoenix

Phoenix Software 07
Balance Sheet
As of March 31, 1997

	Mar 31, '97
ASSETS	
Current Assets	
Checking/Savings	
Bank of Cupertino	80,566.72
Short-term Investments	13,225.00
Total Checking/Savings	93,791.72
Accounts Receivable	
Accounts Receivable	32,139.51
Total Accounts Receivable	32,139.51
Other Current Assets	
Inventory Asset	17,579.40
Investments	14,000.00
Prepaid Insurance	1,038.50
Prepaid Rent	800.00
Undeposited Funds	10,000.00
Total Other Current Assets	43,417.90
Total Current Assets	169,349.13
Fixed Assets	
Computer Equipment	
Cost	28,750.00
Accumulated Depreciation	−375.00
Total Computer Equipment	28,375.00
Furniture	
Cost	3,756.44
Accumulated Depreciation	−313.04
Total Furniture	3,443.40
Total Fixed Assets	31,818.40
TOTAL ASSETS	**201,167.53**
LIABILITIES & EQUITY	
Liabilities	
Current Liabilities	
Accounts Payable	
Accounts Payable	2,199.50
Total Accounts Payable	2,199.50
Other Current Liabilities	
Payroll Liabilities	11,930.57
Sales Tax Payable	7,696.88
Short-Term Debt	5,250.00
Unearned Revenue	4,500.00
Total Other Current Liabilities	29,377.45
Total Current Liabilities	31,576.95
Long Term Liabilities	
Long-Term Debt	86,775.00
Total Long Term Liabilities	86,775.00
Total Liabilities	118,959.32
Equity	
Capital Stock	75,000.00
Net Income	7,815.58
Total Equity	82,815.58
TOTAL LIABILITIES & EQUITY	**201,167.53**

Compare this to Net Income shown on the Income Statement

Next you'll create a balance sheet for the quarter with a column indicating the percentage of total assets for each line item. For example, you'll report the percentage that cash bears to total assets, the percentage that accounts receivable bears to total assets, and so on. To do this you'll use the Customize button to add a new column.

To modify the balance sheet:

1 Click the **Customize** button, then click the **% of Column** check box, then click **OK**.

2 Click the **Format** button, then click the **Show All Numbers Without Cents** check box, then click **OK**.

3 Format the Header by clicking the **Header/Footer** button.

4 Remove the "07" from the header by clicking to the right of the 7 and backspacing twice.

5 Choose **Left** as the Page Layout, then click **OK**.

6 Click the **Print** button, then click **Print** in the Print Reports window to print the report shown in Figure 7.4 on the next page.

7 Close all open windows.

Karen comments that at first she thought the percentage column was the same as the one shown in the income statement: the percentage of total revenue (what QuickBooks calls "income") each item is. But now she sees that this column shows the percentage of total assets. For example, total cash (that is the total amount in checking and savings), is 47% of Phoenix's total assets and accounts receivable is 16% of total assets. She comments that it looks like a large portion of those assets came from long-term debt, as indicated by the 43% long-term debt to assets ratio.

"I wonder if this is what Casey expected for Phoenix's results as of March 31, 1997?" she asks. "Let's compare our actual balance sheet with what Casey budgeted."

To create a budgeted vs. actual balance sheet:

1 Click **Reports, Budget Reports,** then click **Balance Sheet Budget vs. Actual.**

trouble? The balance sheet report created in the prior sequence of steps cannot be modified to include a budget column. Instead you must create a new report from the Budget Reports menu item described in Step 1.

2 Change the report dates from **1/1/97** to **3/31/97** in the Customize Report window.

Phoenix Software 07
Balance Sheet
As of March 31, 1997

Figure 7.4

*A Modified Balance Sheet
for Phoenix*

	Mar 31, '97	% of Column
ASSETS		
Current Assets		
Checking/Savings		
Bank of Cupertino	80,567	40%
Short-term Investments	13,225	7%
Total Checking/Savings	93,792	47%
Accounts Receivable		
Accounts Receivable	32,140	16%
Total Accounts Receivable	32,140	16%
Other Current Assets		
Inventory Asset	17,579	9%
Investments	14,000	7%
Prepaid Insurance	1,039	1%
Prepaid Rent	800	0%
Undeposited Funds	10,000	5%
Total Other Current Assets	43,418	22%
Total Current Assets	169,349	84%
Fixed Assets		
Computer Equipment		
Cost	28,750	14%
Accumulated Depreciation	−375	−0%
Total Computer Equipment	28,375	14%
Furniture		
Cost	3,756	2%
Accumulated Depreciation	−313	−0%
Total Furniture	3,443	2%
Total Fixed Assets	31,818	16%
TOTAL ASSETS	**201,168**	**100%**
LIABILITIES & EQUITY		
Liabilities		
Current Liabilities		
Accounts Payable		
Accounts Payable	2,200	1%
Total Accounts Payable	2,200	1%
Other Current Liabilities		
Payroll Liabilities	11,931	6%
Sales Tax Payable	7,697	4%
Short-Term Debt	5,250	3%
Unearned Revenue	4,500	2%
Total Other Current Liabilities	29,377	15%
Total Current Liabilities	31,577	16%
Long-Term Liabilities		
Long-Term Debt	86,775	43%
Total Long-Term Liabilities	86,775	43%
Total Liabilities	118,959	59%
Equity		
Capital Stock	75,000	37%
Net Income	7,816	4%
Total Equity	82,816	41%
TOTAL LIABILITIES & EQUITY	**201,168**	**100%**

3 Select **Quarter** from the Columns drop-down edit box.

4 Make sure that all check boxes—**Show Actuals**, **and Difference**, and **and % of Budget**—have been checked as shown in Figure 7.5, then click **OK**.

Enter current period dates here

Figure 7.5

Customize Report Window

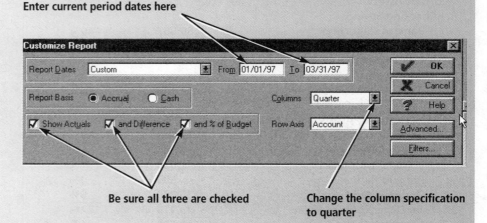

Be sure all three are checked

Change the column specification to quarter

5 Click the **Format** button, then click the **Show All Numbers Without Cents** check box, then click **OK**.

6 Click the **Print** button, click the **Fit report to one page wide** check box, then click **Print** in the Print Reports window to print the report shown in Figure 7.6.

7 Close all windows.

Karen takes the Standard Balance Sheet and the Balance Sheet Budget Comparison to Casey.

"This is very helpful information," he comments as he quickly skims these reports. "I can see Phoenix's financial position, and how we stand in relation to where I thought we'd be. To save time, though, can I see this information expressed in graphical form? I'm afraid I might miss something when I look at this detailed report. A graph would help me see things I might miss when I look at just numbers."

Both you and Karen agree that some graphs would be helpful.

CREATING GRAPHS

In particular, Casey is anxious to know more about his product sales and expenses. It is clear that graphic representations of sales, revenue, and expenses will be helpful.

Figure 7.6 *A Budgeted vs. Actual Balance Sheet for Phoenix*

Phoenix Software 07
Balance Sheet Budget Comparison
As of March 31, 1997

	Mar 31, '97	Budget	$ Over Budget	% of Budget
ASSETS				
Current Assets				
Checking/Savings				
Bank of Cupertino	80,567	33,330	47,237	242%
Short-term Investments	13,225	50,000	−36,775	26%
Total Checking/Savings	93,792	83,330	10,462	113%
Accounts Receivable				
Accounts Receivable	32,140	25,000	7,140	129%
Total Accounts Receivable	32,140	25,000	7,140	129%
Other Current Assets				
Inventory Asset	17,579	40,000	−22,421	44%
Investments	14,000			
Prepaid Insurance	1,039			
Prepaid Rent	800			
Undeposited Funds	10,000			
Total Other Current Assets	43,418	40,000	3,418	109%
Total Current Assets	169,349	148,330	21,019	114%
Fixed Assets				
Computer Equipment				
Cost	28,750	30,000	−1,250	96%
Accumulated Depreciation	−375	400	−25	94%
Total Computer Equipment	28,375	29,600	−1,225	96%
Furniture				
Cost	3,756	3,500	256	107%
Accumulated Depreciation	−313	−300	−13	104%
Total Furniture	3,443	3,200	−243	108%
Total Fixed Assets	31,818	32,800	−982	97%
TOTAL ASSETS	**201,168**	**181,130**	**20,038**	**111%**
LIABILITIES & EQUITY				
Liabilities				
Current Liabilities				
Accounts Payable				
Accounts Payable	2,200	20,000	−17,801	11%
Total Accounts Payable	2,200	20,000	−17,801	11%
Other Current Liabilities				
Payroll Liabilities	11,931	12,000	−69	99%
Sales Tax Payable	7,697	8,000	−303	96%
Short-Term Debt	5,250	10,000	−4,750	53%
Unearned Revenue	4,500			
Total Other Current Liabilities	29,377	30,000	−623	98%
Total Current Liabilities	31,577	50,000	−18,423	63%
Long-Term Liabilities				
Long-Term Debt	86,775	55,000	31,775	158%
Total Long-Term Liabilities	86,775	55,000	31,775	158%
Total Liabilities	118,352	105,000	13,352	113%
Equity				
Capital Stock	75,000	75,000	0	100%
Retained Earnings	0	1,130	−1,130	0%
Net Income	7,816	0	7,816	100%
Total Equity	82,816	76,130	6,686	109%
TOTAL LIABILITIES & EQUITY	**201,168**	**181,130**	**20,038**	**111%**

To create a sales graph:

1 Click **Reports**, then click **Graphs**, then click **Sales**.

2 Click the **Dates** button, and change the dates from **1/1/97** to **3/31/97** in the Change Graph Dates window. Then click **OK**.

3 Click the **By Item** button in the QuickInsight Sales Graphs window, if it is not already selected. Selecting this button causes QuickBooks to display sales in the graph by item, in this case by the hardware and the services that Phoenix sells.

4 QuickBooks generates two graphs—a bar chart and a pie chart—as shown in Figure 7.7. Study these graphs.

Figure 7.7

A Sales by Month Graph for Phoenix—By Item

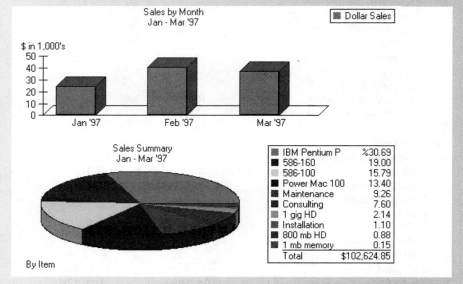

5 Click the **By Customer** button in the QuickInsight Sales Graphs window to create a graph that illustrates sales for the quarter by customer. See Figure 7.8.

Figure 7.8

A Sales by Month Graph for Phoenix—By Customer

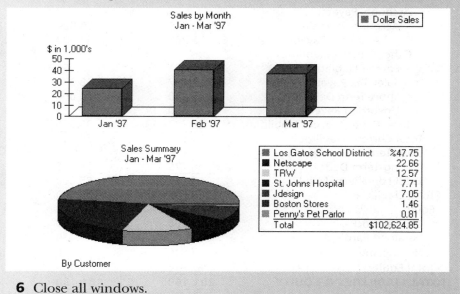

6 Close all windows.

Graphs such as these help managers interpret financial information, because they often reveal important relationships not obvious from the financial statements. For example, in Figure 7.8, sales growth by month is illustrated and the source of sales by customer is revealed. In this case Los Gatos School District represents almost 48% of sales for the quarter.

Next you decide to produce a graph that illustrates Phoenix's revenues (or "income" as QuickBooks calls it) and expenses.

To create a revenue and expense graph:

1 Click **Reports**, then click **Graphs**, then click **Income & Expenses**.

2 Click the **Dates** button, and change the dates from **1/1/97** to **3/31/97** in the Change Graph Dates window. Then click **OK**.

3 Click the **By Account** button and the **Expense** button in the QuickInsight Sales Graphs window, if they are not already selected.

4 The graph shown in Figure 7.9 appears. Study this graph.

trouble? Your vertical axis scale might be different, depending on the size of the figure you choose to view.

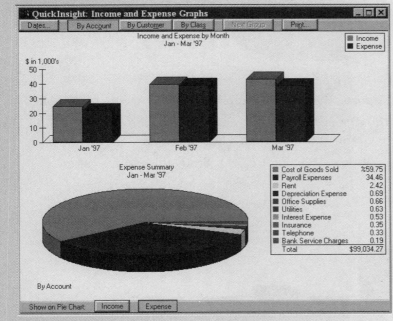

Figure 7.9

An Income (Revenue) and Expense by Month Graph for Phoenix Systems, Including Details of Expenses for the Quarter

5 Close all windows.

These two graphs help to explain revenues and expenses, but they do not provide insight into the financial position of the company as of March 31.

"Does QuickBooks have similar graphing capabilities for items such as accounts receivable and accounts payable?" Karen asks.

"Yes," you respond. "In fact, we should probably create a graph for both accounts to demonstrate how current or noncurrent our receivables and payables are. QuickBooks can create a bar chart that illustrates aging for accounts receivable and then another for accounts payable, and simultaneously identify who owes us or who we owe, respectively, at any single time, such as March 31, 1997."

To create accounts receivable and accounts payable graphs:

1 Click **Reports**, then click **Graphs**, then click **Accounts Receivable**.

2 Click the **Dates** button and change the date to **3/31/97** in the Change Graph Dates window. Then click **OK**.

3 A graph appears. See Figure 7.10. Study this figure.

Figure 7.10

A Graph Illustrating the Aging of Accounts Receivable and Customer Balances

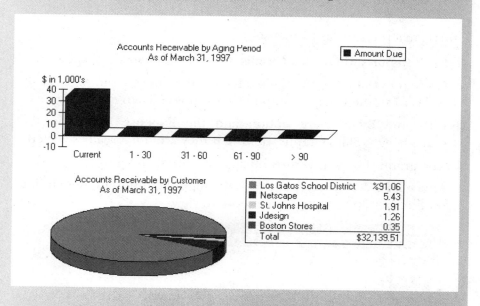

4 Click **Reports**, then click **Graphs**, then click **Accounts Payable**.

5 Click the **Dates** button and change the date to **3/31/97** in the Change Graph Dates window. Then click **OK**.

6 A graph appears. See Figure 7.11. Study this figure.

Figure 7.11

A Graph Illustrating the Aging of Accounts Payable and Vendor Balances

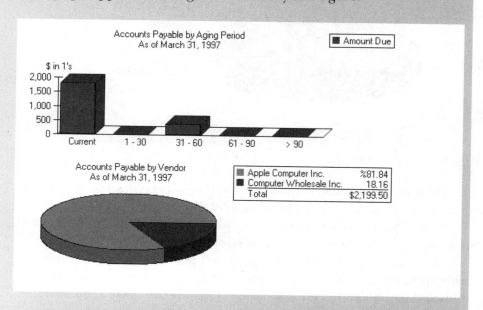

7 Close all windows.

When you show Casey these graphs, he comments that they will be very helpful. But he wants to see even more information derived from the financial statements—specifically, he wants to see reports on sales, purchases, and inventory.

CREATING ADDITIONAL REPORTS

With QuickBooks you can generate many supporting reports for the financial statements—what accountants consider traditional support in the form of schedules.

Karen reads through QuickBooks Help and discovers two reports that QuickBooks generates that will help Casey—the Sales by Customer Summary and the Summary Sales by Item. Together you decide that the Sales by Customer Summary should identify sales for each month of the quarter so you can see to which customers you sold product or services. The Summary Sales by Item reports on the number of items sold, the average price of each item sold, and each item's related average cost. This report also identifies the gross margin (sales revenue minus cost of goods sold) amount for each item and summarizes the gross margin for all items sold during the period. Karen suggests that you produce this report on a quarterly basis.

To create the Sales by Customer Summary and the Summary Sales by Item reports:

1 Click **Reports**, then click **Sales Reports**, then click **By Customer Summary**.

2 Change the report dates from **1/1/97** to **3/31/97** in the Customize Report window.

3 Select **Month** from the Columns drop-down edit box, then click **OK**. The report shown in Figure 7.12 appears.

Figure 7.12
Sales by Customer by Month

Phoenix Software 07
Sales by Customer Summary
January through March 1997

	Jan '97	Feb '97	Mar '97	TOTAL
Boston Stores	0.00	0.00	1,500.00	1,500.00
Jdesign	640.00	6,590.00	0.00	7,230.00
Los Gatos School District	17,125.00	0.00	31,875.00	49,000.00
Netscape	0.00	20,250.00	3,000.00	23,250.00
Penny's Pet Parlor	0.00	834.85	0.00	834.85
St. Johns Hospital	6,875.00	0.00	1,035.00	7,910.00
TRW	0.00	12,900.00	0.00	12,900.00
TOTAL	24,640.00	40,574.85	37,410.00	102,624.85

4 Click **Reports**, then click **Sales Reports**, then click **By Item Summary**.

5 Change the report dates from **1/1/97** to **3/31/97** in the Customize Report window.

6 Select **Total Only** from the Columns drop-down edit box, then click **OK**.

7 Adjust the column width to view more of the report on your screen as shown in Figure 7.13. Scroll down the report to view items sold and total sales.

Figure 7.13
Sales by Item for the Quarter

Phoenix Software 07
Summary Sales by Item
January through March 1997

	Qty	Amount	% of Sales	Avg Price	COGS	Avg COGS	Gross Mar...	Gross Margin %
Inventory								
1 gig HD	4	2,200.00	2.1%	550.00	1,800.00	450.00	400.00	18.2%
1 mb memory	3	149.85	0.1%	49.95	119.85	39.95	30.00	20%
586-100	9	16,200.00	15.8%	1,800.00	13,500.00	1,500.00	2,700.00	16.7%
586-160	5	19,500.00	19%	3,900.00	11,500.00	2,300.00	8,000.00	41%
800 mb HD	3	900.00	0.9%	300.00	750.00	250.00	150.00	16.7%
IBM Pentium P	3	31,500.00	30.7%	10,500.00	22,500.00	7,500.00	9,000.00	28.6%
Power Mac 100	5	13,750.00	13.4%	2,750.00	9,000.00	1,800.00	4,750.00	34.5%
Total Inventory		84,199.85	82%		59,169.85		25,030.00	29.7%
Service								
Consulting	104	7,800.00	7.6%	75.00				
Installation	25	1,125.00	1.1%	45.00				
Maintenance	190	9,500.00	9.3%	50.00				
Total Service		18,425.00	18%					
TOTAL		102,624.85	100.0%					

8 Close all windows.

Karen tells you that three additional reports are commonly prepared to support the balance sheet for the quarter: an accounts receivable aging, an accounts payable aging, and an inventory status report. QuickBooks can easily generate these reports.

To create an Accounts Receivable Aging report:

1 Click **Reports**, then click **A/R Reports**, then click **Aging Summary**.

2 Change the Through date to **3/31/97** in the Customize Report window, then click **OK**. The report shown in Figure 7.14 appears. Examine this report.

3 Did you notice a negative $1,000 amount on the Boston Stores line? To investigate, double-click the **–1,000**.

4 When the A/R Aging QuickZoom window appears, double-click the **3/06/97** payment.

5 The Receive Payments window appears showing a payment of $2,500, of which only $1,500 was applied to open invoices. Now you remember that the balance of $1,000 was transferred to Unearned Revenue (a liability account) for the balance sheet disclosure.

Note the -1,000.00 amount

Phoenix Software 07
A/R Aging Summary
As of March 31, 1997

	Current	1 - 30	31 - 60	61 - 90	> 90	TOTAL
Boston Stores	1,112.50	-1,000.00	0.00	0.00	0.00	112.50
Jdesign	0.00	405.00	0.00	0.00	0.00	405.00
Los Gatos School District	29,265.63	0.00	0.00	0.00	0.00	29,265.63
Netscape	3,725.00	1,518.75	0.00	-3,500.00	0.00	1,743.75
St. Johns Hospital	0.00	612.63	0.00	0.00	0.00	612.63
TOTAL	34,103.13	1,536.38	0.00	-3,500.00	0.00	32,139.51

Figure 7.14

Accounts Receivable Aging Report

6 Click **Reports**, then click **A/P Reports**, then click **Aging Summary**.

7 Change the Through date to **3/31/97** in the Customize Report window, then click **OK** to view the report shown in Figure 7.15.

Phoenix Software 07
A/P Aging Summary
As of March 31, 1997

	Current	1 - 30	31 - 60	61 - 90	> 90	TOTAL
Apple Computer Inc.	1,800.00	0.00	0.00	0.00	0.00	1,800.00
Computer Wholesale Inc.	0.00	0.00	399.50	0.00	0.00	399.50
TOTAL	1,800.00	0.00	399.50	0.00	0.00	2,199.50

Figure 7.15

Accounts Payable Aging Report

8 Click **Reports**, then click **Inventory Reports**, then click **Stock Status by Item**.

9 Change the From date to **1/1/97** and the Through date to **3/31/97** in the Customize Report window, then click **OK** to view the report, a portion of which is shown in Figure 7.16. Scroll to the right to view the remaining report.

Phoenix Software 07
Inventory Stock Status by Item
January through March 1997

	Item Description	Pref Vendor	Reor...	On Hand
1 gig HD	1,000mb Bengal Hard Disk	Bengal Drives, Inc		4
1 mb memory	Memory modules	Computer Wholesale Inc.	20	12
586-100	Phoenix Pentium Computer - 100 mhz	Computer Wholesale Inc.		1
586-160	Phoenix 586 160 Megahertz	Computer Wholesale Inc.	3	5
800 mb HD	800mb Bengal Hard Disk	Bengal Drives, Inc		2
IBM Pentium P	IBM Pentium Plus Computers	IBM		0
Power Mac 100	Apple Power Mac 100	Apple Computer Inc.	4	1

Figure 7.16

Inventory Stock Status by Item

10 Close all windows.

END NOTE

. . . .

You've completed the reports for Casey and decide to deliver them to his office. After quickly skimming each report, Casey compliments you both on your fine work and you turn to walk back to your office.

As you walk back to your office, Karen comments, "That's the first time I've ever created financial statements without using debits and credits. How is that possible?"

"All the debits and credits are done for you," you explain. "Tomorrow I'll show you that QuickBooks in fact still keeps data in a debit and credit format and can provide the traditional general ledger, journal entries, and trial balance procedures you are more familiar with."

practice

Chapter 7 Questions

1 Explain how you can use QuickBooks to customize any report.

2 What are the optional columns available in the Customize Report window when you create a balance sheet?

3 What time periods are available for the columns of a balance sheet?

4 What options are available in the Format Report window for a balance sheet?

5 How do you resize a report that would normally print on two pages to one page?

6 When you create a balance sheet, what result does clicking the Collapse button have?

7 What different graphs are available in QuickBooks?

8 Discuss why percentage changes identified in the budgeted vs. actual reports need to be interpreted carefully.

9 Describe the information available in the accounts receivable and accounts payable aging reports.

10 Describe the information available in the inventory stocks status report.

Chapter 7 Assignments

1 *Creating Financial Reports and Supporting Schedules for Phoenix Systems, Inc.*

Using phnx07.qbw from your Student Disk, create and print the following reports:

   a. an income statement for the month ended January 31, 1997
   b. a balance sheet as of January 31, 1997
   c. a budgeted income statement vs. actual income statement for the month ended January 31, 1997
   d. a budgeted balance sheet vs. actual balance sheet as of January 31, 1997
   e. a sales by customer summary for the month ended January 31, 1997
   f. a sales by item summary for the month ended January 31, 1997
   g. an accounts receivable aging report as of January 31, 1997
   h. an accounts payable aging report as of January 31, 1997
   i. an inventory valuation summary as of January 31, 1997

2 *Creating Graphs for Phoenix Systems, Inc.*

Using phnx07.qbw from your Student Disk, create and print the following graphs:

   a. sales for the month ended January 31, 1997
   b. revenue (income) and expense for the month ended January 31, 1997
   c. accounts receivable aging as of January 31, 1997
   d. accounts payable aging as of January 31, 1997

3 *Using the South-Western Home Page for More Assignments or Cases*

If you have Internet access, go to the home page for this textbook at owen.swcollege.com.

Select the **Chapter 7** section, and complete the problem(s) assigned by your instructor.

http://
Go to
owen.swcollege.com

Chapter 7 Case Problem: JENNINGS & ASSOCIATES—Financial Reports and Graphs

Now that the budget data and related adjustments have been made, Kelly can create and print the appropriate reports and graphs.

Use kj07cp.qbw from your Student Disk. (*Note:* Additional transactions have been included in this file that were not included in Chapter 6. Do not use your completed kj06cp.qbw file.)

1 Create and print the following reports using proper headings. Use a left page layout, and format the report without cents.

   a. an income statement for the quarter ended March 31, 1997
   b. a balance sheet as of March 31, 1997
   c. a balance sheet showing budgeted vs. actual amounts with $ Over Budget and % of Budget columns as of March 31, 1997 (*Hint:* Display only the month of March.)
   d. an income statement showing budgeted vs. actual amounts with $ Over Budget and % of Budget columns for the quarter ended March 31, 1997
   e. a sales by customer summary for the quarter ended March 31, 1997
   f. a sales by item summary for the quarter ended March 31, 1997
   g. an accounts receivable aging summary report as of March 31, 1997
   h. an accounts payable aging summary report as of March 31, 1997
   i. an inventory valuation summary as of March 31, 1997 in landscape view.

2 Create and print the following graphs:

   a. sales for the quarter ended March 31, 1997
   b. revenue (income) and expense for the quarter ended March 31, 1997
   c. accounts receivable aging as of March 31, 1997
   d. accounts payable aging as of March 31, 1997

appendix

Debits and Credits

In this appendix you will:

- Prepare a trial balance
- Examine a general ledger
- Examine a journal entry used to record a business transaction
- Journalize a transaction

CASE: PHOENIX SYSTEMS CONSULTING,INC.

You and Karen have been recording business transactions for Phoenix without using journal entries or mentioning the terms *debit* and *credit* even once. This is another one of the benefits of using QuickBooks: It enables businesspeople who were not accounting majors to "do accounting." Moreover accountants appreciate QuickBooks, because they can use it with clients who want to have more control over their finances but who do not have formal accounting training.

As a user of QuickBooks, you should know that although you haven't actually used debits and credits in this book, QuickBooks is based on a dual-entry or double-entry accounting system. Every transaction that you entered in Chapters 2 through 7 had an effect on two or more accounts in the chart of accounts. For example, every sales invoice increased Sales Revenue and Accounts Receivable. Every time you initiated a QuickBooks activity such as "receive payments," Cash was increased and Accounts Receivable was decreased.

QuickBooks actually provides three equivalent ways for you to record transactions using the double-entry system: You can record transactions by using business documents (what QuickBooks refers to as Forms), by using registers, or by making journal entries. In this textbook so far, you have used documents and registers. Recall that using a document involves recording a transaction by completing a business document, such as a sales invoice or a check. When you correctly complete the document, the effect(s) of the transaction on the financial statements are automatically entered. For example, when Phoenix paid its yearly insurance premium of $1,384.67 on 1/7/97, the dual effects of this transaction on the Prepaid Insurance account (increased) and the Cash account (decreased) were processed by filling out a business document, specifically a check. In contrast, using registers involves accessing a particular account's register and inputting the effects of the transaction. For example, you could choose either the Prepaid Insurance register or the Bank of Cupertino (cash) register and enter the changes (increase/decrease) as needed.

Karen asks if it is possible, however, to still use debits and credits in QuickBooks, because her formal accounting training focused primarily on journal entries as the source of every transaction. You explain that, yes, it is indeed possible, and you offer to demonstrate QuickBooks's ability to prepare a trial balance, a general ledger, and a journal entry. You point out that under normal circumstances, you would begin the accounting process with a journal entry. In this case, however, you will view the steps with her in reverse order, because the process has already been completed.

TRIAL BALANCE

The trial balance is a two-column listing of all asset, liability, owners' equity, revenue, and expense accounts. Accounts that have debit balances are listed in the debit column, and accounts that have credit balances are listed in the credit column. Although not foolproof, an equality between debits and credits generally indicates that the accounting process has been followed correctly.

With QuickBooks you can quickly create a trial balance. All you need is the date as of which you want the trial balance. Then you can use QuickBooks's QuickZoom feature to view supporting accounts and supporting journals or business documents.

To create the trial balance and examine supporting detail:

1 Open phnx07.qbw located on your Student Disk.

2 Click **Reports**, **Other Reports**, then **Trial Balance**.

3 Change the report dates from **1/1/97** to **3/31/97** in the Customize Report window, then click **OK** to view the trial balance you have prepared, as shown in Figure A.1

Figure A.1
Trial Balance

Phoenix Software 07
Trial Balance
As of March 31, 1997

	Mar 31, '97	
	Debit	Credit
Bank of Cupertino	80,566.72	
Short-term Investments	13,225.00	
Accounts Receivable	32,139.51	
Inventory Asset	17,579.40	
Investments	14,000.00	
Prepaid Insurance	1,038.50	
Prepaid Rent	800.00	
Undeposited Funds	10,000.00	
Computer Equipment:Cost	28,750.00	
Computer Equipment:Accumulated Depreciation		375.00
Furniture:Cost	3,756.44	
Furniture:Accumulated Depreciation		313.04

Double-click here to view the Prepaid Insurance account

4 Double-click on the **1,038.50 Prepaid Insurance** amount to view the Prepaid Insurance account shown in Figure A.2.

5 Double-click on the **−346.17 Prepaid Insurance** amount to view the Prepaid Insurance account, then double-click the word GENJRNL to view the Prepaid Insurance adjusting journal entry shown in Figure A.3. Recall that this adjusting journal entry increases an expense and decreases an asset.

6 Close all windows.

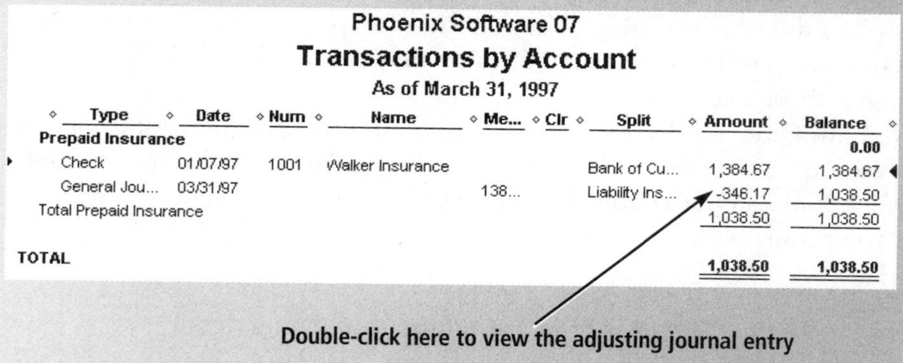

Figure A.2
General Ledger Account

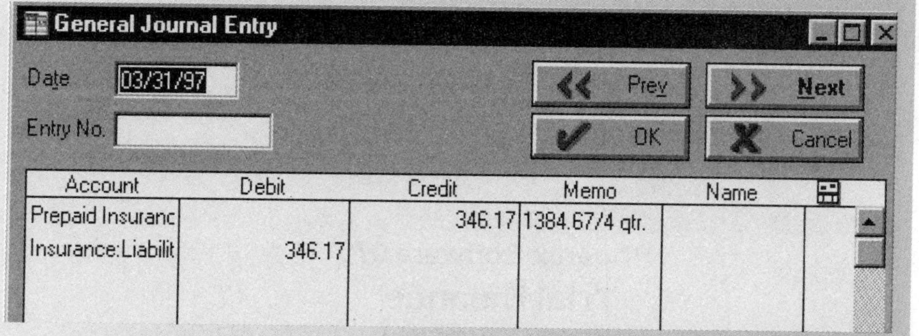

Phoenix Software 07
Transactions by Account
As of March 31, 1997

Type	Date	Num	Name	Me...	Clr	Split	Amount	Balance
Prepaid Insurance								0.00
Check	01/07/97	1001	Walker Insurance			Bank of Cu...	1,384.67	1,384.67
General Jou...	03/31/97			138...		Liability Ins...	-346.17	1,038.50
Total Prepaid Insurance							1,038.50	1,038.50
TOTAL							1,038.50	1,038.50

Double-click here to view the adjusting journal entry

Figure A.3
General Journal Entry

General Journal Entry

Date 03/31/97   Prev   Next
Entry No.   OK   Cancel

Account	Debit	Credit	Memo	Name	
Prepaid Insuranc		346.17	1384.67/4 qtr.		
Insurance:Liabilit	346.17				

The journal entry shown in Figure A.3 was actually created by entering an adjustment to an account register. The adjustment itself was not a standard transaction entry prompted by the existence of a business source document, such as a check, an invoice, or a bill. Instead it was necessary for Casey to anticipate its recording at the end of March.

GENERAL LEDGER

The general ledger is used in accounting information systems to store the effects of individual asset, liability, owners' equity, revenue, and expense accounts. In manual accounting systems, journals are used to record business transactions, the effects of which are then posted or transferred to a general ledger. This recording and posting is compressed into one step in QuickBooks as the transactions are recorded. You decide to use a sales invoice to demonstrate to Karen how the effects of a transaction are stored in the general ledger.

You explain to her that the invoice itself is used as a source business document. Information is entered into the invoice and when you click OK, the invoice is stored and the consequence of that invoice is immediately recorded. In accounting jargon, once you enter the invoice, a debit is posted to the Accounts Receivable account in the general ledger and a credit is posted to the Sales Revenue account in the general ledger.

"In my accounting classes we usually posted all the sales for a month with one journal entry," Karen comments. "In this case, it looks like each sale is recorded individually. Doesn't that take a lot of time?"

"Yes, " you agree. "But once you enter this invoice, several steps are completed simultaneously. Accounts Receivable is debited and Sales Revenue is credited. If we're selling inventory, the same invoice updates the perpetual inventory record, credits the Inventory account, and debits the Cost of Goods Sold account. Plus, the customer's account is adjusted accordingly so we know how much each customer owes and when amounts are due. Let's take a look at QuickBooks's general ledger and some underlying transactions."

To create the general ledger:

1 Click **Reports, Other Reports**, then **General Ledger**.

2 Change the report dates from **1/1/97** to **3/31/97** in the Customize Report window, then click **OK** to view the general ledger, as shown in Figure A.4.

Figure A.4

Phoenix's General Ledger

Phoenix Software 07
General Ledger
As of March 31, 1997

Type	Date	Num	Name	Memo	Split	Amount
Bank of Cupertino						
Deposit	01/02/97			Deposit	Capital Stock	25,000.00
Check	01/07/97	1001	Walker Insurance		Prepaid Insur...	-1,384.67
Check	01/08/97	1002	E-Max Realty	First and las...	Prepaid Rent	-1,600.00
Check	01/09/97	1003	Apple Computer Inc.		Inventory As...	-9,000.00
Deposit	01/10/97			Deposit	Capital Stock	50,000.00
Deposit	01/10/97			Transfer	Short-term In...	-8,000.00
Cash Sale	01/13/97	501	St. Johns Hospital		-SPLIT-	2,015.63
Check	01/13/97	1004	Sky Investments		Investments	-40,000.00
Check	01/14/97	1005	Bengal Drives, Inc		Inventory As...	-2,250.00
Cash Sale	01/14/97	502	Jdesign		-SPLIT-	688.00
Payment	01/14/97		Netscape		Accounts Re...	6,500.00

3 Scroll down to display the Prepaid Insurance and Prepaid Rent general ledger accounts as shown in Figure A.5.

4 Double-click on the **–346.17 Prepaid Insurance** amount to view the Prepaid Insurance account, then double-click the word GENJRNL to view the Prepaid Insurance adjusting journal entry as you did before.

5 Click on **Insurance:liabili.** Note in Figure A.6 that this adjustment includes a debit to Liability Insurance, an expense account, and a credit to Prepaid Insurance, another current asset account.

6 Close all windows.

Phoenix Software 07

10/29/96

General Ledger

As of March 31, 1997

◊ Type ◊	Date ◊	Num ◊	Name ◊	Memo ◊	Split ◊	Amount
Prepaid Insurance						
Check	01/07/97	1001	Walker Insurance		Bank of Cupe...	1,384.67
General ...	03/31/97			1384.67/4 qtr.	Liability Insur...	-346.17
Total Prepaid Insurance						1,038.50
Prepaid Rent						
Check	01/08/97	1002	E-Max Realty	First and las...	Bank of Cupe...	1,600.00
General ...	03/31/97				Rent	-800.00
Total Prepaid Rent						800.00

Double-click here to view the journal

Click here first to reveal the drop-down arrow

Then click the drop-down arrow to view a list of accounts

General Journal Entry

Date 03/31/97   **Next**

Entry No.   ✔ OK   ✗ Cancel

Account	Debit	Credit	Memo	Name	
Prepaid Insuranc		346.17	1384.67/4 qtr.		
Insurance:Lia	346.17				

Insurance	Expense
Disability Insurance	Expense
✓ Liability Insurance	Expense
Work Comp	Expense
Interest Expense	Expense
Finance Charge	Expense
Loan Interest	Expense
Mortgage	Expense
Licenses and Permits	Expense
Miscellaneous	Expense
Office Supplies	Expense
Outside Services	Expense

After seeing how easy this is, you might wonder why QuickBooks—or some other similar program— isn't used all the time in business. The reason is that many companies often have their own accounting software that has been customized to their specifications. However, many smaller businesses, which often can't afford such a luxury as customized software, have found QuickBooks to be an inexpensive, yet powerful and easy-to-use alternative.

JOURNALIZING AN ADJUSTMENT

Another way to record adjustments—other than through an account's register—is to enter a transaction with a journal entry using the QuickBooks activity known as "entering special transactions." You decide to show this approach to Karen by recording next quarter's depreciation.

To record an adjustment using a journal entry:

1 Click **Activities**, then **Make Journal Entry**.

2 Change the date to **6/30/97**, then enter the Journal Entry No. **101**.

3 Click in the upper part of the Account column, then click on the drop-down edit arrow to select a debit account: **Depreciation Expense**.

4 Click in the Debit column across from the Depreciation Expense account; then enter **500**.

5 Click in the Account column below Depreciation Expense, then click on the drop-down edit arrow to select a credit account: **Furniture:Accumulated Depreciation**. Note that a $500 amount is automatically entered in the Credit column across from the Accumulated Depreciation account.

6 Click at the top of the Memo column, then enter **Depreciation for the 2ⁿᵈ quarter**.

7 Maximize the General Journal Entry window to view the screen shown in Figure A.7.

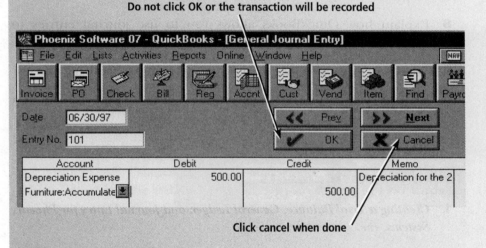

Figure A.7
Sample General Journal Entry

8 Do *not* click OK. Instead click **Cancel**.

END NOTE

Many accountants prefer to use journal entries (that is the debit-credit format) to record business transactions. But Intuit Inc. designed QuickBooks for businesspeople who did not want to use journal entries. Although QuickBooks allows you to enter all transactions using the journal entry format, you then must sacrifice QuickBooks's specialized invoicing, bill payment, payroll, and other useful features. The choice is yours!

practice

Appendix Questions

1 In what order does QuickBooks list accounts in the trial balance report?

2 What QuickBooks feature allows you to access supporting accounts or journals when viewing the trial balance?

3 What happens when you double-click an amount on the trial balance?

4 Explain how a transaction recorded through an account register also creates a general journal entry.

5 Why does QuickBooks have a general ledger?

6 What advantages does QuickBooks's document initiated recording method have over the standard journal entry method?

7 What happens when you double-click on an amount in the general ledger?

8 Explain how QuickBooks allows you to use journal entries to record business transactions.

9 What activity would you use to access QuickBooks's journal entries?

10 Explain how accounts are accessed when you enter information into QuickBooks's general journal entry window.

Appendix Assignments

1 *Creating a Trial Balance, General Ledger, and Journal Entry for Phoenix Systems, Inc.*

Use phnx07.qbw from your Student Disk to do a through c:

a. Create and print a trial balance as of February 28, 1997.
b. Create and print page 1 of the general ledger as of February 28, 1997 in landscape view.
c. Locate the journal entry that amortized one month's rent expense in March 1997.

2 *Using the South-Western Home Page for More Assignments or Cases*

If you have Internet access, go to the home page for this textbook at owen.swcollege.com.

Select the **Appendix** section, and complete the problem(s) your instructor assigns.

http://

Go to
owen.swcollege.com

Appendix Case: JENNINGS & ASSOCIATES—Debits and Credits

Kelly has hired an outside accountant to review her financial statements. The accountant has asked for a trial balance and a general ledger, and Kelly asks you to prepare them.

Use kj07cp.qbw on your Student Disk.

a. Create and print a trial balance as of March 31, 1997.

b. Create and print page 1 of the general ledger for the quarter ended March 31, 1997 in landscape view.

Index